VLA FLV VIVS

# The Old Town
# and the Royal Castle
# in Warsaw

The Old Town and the Royal Castle · *Jan Zachwatowicz*

The Reconstruction of the Old Town · *Piotr Biegański*

The History of the Royal Castle · *Stanisław Lorentz*

The Reconstruction of the Royal Castle · *Aleksander Gieysztor*

Colour photographs by *Krzysztof Jabłoński*

Translated by *Jerzy A. Bałdyga*

With compliments
National Tourist Enterprise
ORBIS

# The Old Town and the Royal Castle in Warsaw

Arkady

p. I of the jacket – View of the Royal Castle from Świętojańska Street
p. IV of the jacket – View of the Barbican from Podwale Street
Front-paper – View of Warsaw from the end of the 16th century
End-paper – View of Warsaw by Zygmunt Vogel from the end of the 18th century

Graphic design · *Stefan Bernaciński*

Photographs by C. Olszewski (11, 22), A. Pietrzak (19), H. Poddębski (20, 21), S. Proszowski (23), B. Rogaliński (95, 102, 111, 122, 123), H. Romanowski (16, 17), L. Sempoliński (10), B. Seredyńska (18), S. Sobkowicz (4), W. Stasiak (28), H. Śmigacz (8, 9) and W. Wolny (7)

Captions to illustrations · *Bożena Wierzbicka*
Editors · *Bożena Wierzbicka, Maria Łotyszowa*
Technical editor · *Bogumiła Sajek*

© Copyright by Arkady, Warsaw 1988

ISBN 83-213-3527-6
(ISBN 83-213-3357-5 1st edit.)

*For the Poles, the Royal Castle in Warsaw is a symbol of the Nation and the State, of the struggle for independence and resistance against the Nazi invaders. Exactly because of this symbolic meaning, Hitler had this former seat of Polish kings completely razed to the ground. The reconstruction of the Castle has been a matter of nation – wide importance, uniting all the Poles. When the enemy destroyed the Castle, we tried to save from it as much as we could – for we were certain that the victory would be ours and that the Castle would be rebuilt.*

*In those terrible autumn months of 1939, the idea of the reconstruction was born – now we are fulfilling the will of those who at risk to their lives fought for the works of Polish culture.*

*The last dramatic and heroic chapter in the history of the Castle has been its reconstruction by the efforts of Poles from all over the world. This has given the Royal Castle in Warsaw the force of expression of a new symbol. We should like the reborn Castle to be a Monument of National History and Culture, a place of solemn state and national acts, particularly important scientific and cultural meetings and solemn congresses of people of Polish origin from abroad, making one realize that all Poles, those who live in Poland and those who are scattered over the different continents, form one Nation, attached to its historical traditions and filled with love for the Fatherland.*

*Stanisław Lorentz*

# The Old Town and the Royal Castle

*Jan Zachwatowicz*

The earliest settlement in the area of present-day Warsaw, uncovered by archaeological excavations, dates back to the period of the Lusatian culture. Even in the early Middle Ages (in the 10th and 11th centuries), there was a large number of settlements, which were located on the lower, right bank of the Vistula or at lower parts of the left bank. In the 13th century, particular significance was acquired by a settlement called Jazdów, situated at a ford across the river, and known already as a stronghold. It was not until the end of the 13th century that a settlement and a stronghold arose on the high left bank of the Vistula, at the place where the Old Town and the Castle now stand.

The stronghold arose as the seat of a castellan at the turn of the 13th and 14th centuries, founded by the Mazovian duke, and, in the 14th century, it became the duke's castle. It was situated in the south part of the new settlement area, in the direct vicinity of the urban settlement. At the beginning of the 14th century the town and the stronghold were surrounded by earthen-wooden ramparts with two gates: the Court (Dworzańska, later Cracow) Gate from the south and the Bath (Łaziebna, later New Town) Gate from the north.

In the 30's of the 14th century, the town, already built up and fortified, was vibrant with life. In 1338–1339, the famous court case against the Teutonic Order took place in Warsaw. In the Market Place a masonry town hall arose, masonry houses were erected. Within the ramparts, masonry gates were built. In the second half of the 14th century, the earthen-wooden ramparts were replaced by a defensive wall, which also ran, on the east side, towards the Vistula. The wall had twelve rectangular towers, two gates and two wicket doors from the side of the Vistula. In

*1. The first preserved view of Warsaw in the "Constitution of the Warsaw General Parliament... 1581"*

7

the northeast corner a tall masonry tower (called later the Marshall's Tower) was erected. In the south part the fortifications of the town connected with the walls of the Castle, where, the duke's house – Curia Maior arose.

In the 14th century two churches were built in the area of the town. They were the parish church of St. John and the Augustinian church of St. Martin with a monastery. In the 15th century, north of the Old Town, a large urban settlement developed – this was the New Town with a spacious rectangular market place. It was not surrounded by fortifications. South of the Old Town, a Bernardine monastery with St. Ann's church arose. At the beginning of the 15th century, work was begun on the construction of the second line of defensive walls surrounding the Old Town. These walls, displaced before the 14th-century ramparts, had eleven semicircular towers. In the early 16th century, a new additional gate (called the Side Gate), crowned with an attic wall, was built. In front of the New Town Gate, a gothic, two-arcaded defensive bridge, with towers on the pendentives, complete with a barbican crowned with an attic wall, was erected. A similar bridge led to the Cracow Gate.

*2. Detail of the view of Warsaw by Christian Melich (?), about 1630*

*3. Detail of the view of Warsaw by Erik Dahlberg, from 1656*

URBS WARSOVIA
Sedes Ordinaria Regum
Poloniæ ea facie exhibita qua con
spiciebatur postquam amisso prælio
à Ser. R. Poloniæ deserta et à S.R.M.
Sueciæ secunda vice occupata
fuit d. 22. Iul. An. 1656.

Templum Bernhar-
dinorum
Suburbia exusta
Regis Sigismun-
di statua
Templum Monialium
S. Claræ
Arx Regia
Templum
Augustin
Temp. S. Iohannis
Templum et Colleg:
Iesuitarum
Curia
Palat. Principis
Caroli Ferdinandi
Mons Fimi

A
F L U

The Old Town town hall was also expanded. The 16th century brought changes which would significantly affect the fate of Warsaw. In 1526, after the death of the last Mazovian duke, the Castle became royal property. The King Sigismund Augustus undertook construction work at the Castle, adding to the former edifice of the Curia Maior a new manor, connected with the gothic building of the Curia Minor. Rooms with one, two and three pillars date from this period.

In 1569, the Castle, already then the Royal Castle, became the seat of legislative authority – the Parliament of the Commonwealth. Soon, in the neighbourhood of the Old Town and the Castle, magnates' and noblemen's residences – magnificent palaces with gardens – and the houses of merchants and craftsmen, coming in great numbers to Warsaw, arose. New settlements were formed, called jurisdictions, ruling themselves independently of the town authorities of the Old Warsaw. There was a significant change in proportions between the building of the Old Town, with its 160 houses, and that of the suburbs, with its 500 houses.

*4. Detail of the view of Warsaw by Bernardo Bellotto called Canaletto from 1770*

In 1596, the King Sigismund III Vasa, established Warsaw finally as the capital and began a reconstruction of the Castle. The work took many years and was continued by King Ladislaus IV in the 30's of the 17th century.

The town rapidly gained territory. In 1621–1624, a new line of bastion fortifications arose, which surrounded the main part of the town with its palaces, houses and monasteries, but the new settlements and jurisdictions were formed outside of this fortification line. At the Old Town Market Place houses with early baroque elevations were built. During the Swedish wars Warsaw and its Old Town were to a large extent destroyed. The Royal Castle, damaged and looted, also suffered.

After the war the residences and the Old Town were rebuilt, and new elevations were introduced in a large number of houses. It was not until the 70's of the 17th century, during the reign of King John III Sobieski, that the work at the castle was carried out. In the early 18th century, the Palace Under the Tin Roof arose south of the Castle. In 1703 Warsaw was again occupied by the Swedes and the Castle was looted. The King, Augustus II, used only some of the castle interiors. He commissioned designs to be made of a new royal residence in the place of the former Morsztyn Manor. At the same time, modifications were carried out at the Castle. The work was interrupted by the 1732 fire at the Castle. Augustus III took over the conception of a thorough rebuilding of the Castle; the design versions were made by Saxon architects. The construction work was carried out in 1741–1746. Further modifications of the Castle, undertaken on the initiative of King Stanislaus Augustus, were carried out in 1763–1788 by Jakub Fontana, Jan Chrystian Kamsetzer and Domenico Merlini. It was then that the magnificent interiors of Stanislaus halls, filled with works of art, and the King's Library, set over the north wing of the Palace Under the Tin Roof, arose.

The loss of independence began the long and dramatic history of the Castle. The Prussians took away a large part of its furnishings. Modifications were begun in the interiors. In 1817, work was begun on the demolition of the buildings of the courtyard in front of the Castle, on the Grodzka Street side, including the Cracow Gate. A square arose to the west, in front of the Castle. In the same year the town hall in the Old Town was demolished. The Old Town had also finally lost its significance, becoming a small residential district. The composition of the Old Town population also changed. The seats of patrician families were taken over by the poor, cooped up in the increasingly built up Old Town blocks, which had taken over the remains of the former fortifications.

After the November Uprising, from 1832 on, the Castle collections were gradually taken away to Russia. The Castle became the seat of the Russian governors-general. It also housed barracks. At that time, the immediate surroundings of the Castle changed. After the Bernardine church and convent were demolished in 1843, a downhill road was built between Castle Square and the bridge erected in 1864 by the engineer Stanisław Kierbedź. In the Old Town a new small square – Zapiecek – was formed in the place of a house which had collapsed. Butcher's stalls and shops

5. *View of Warsaw by Zygmunt Vogel from the end of the 18th century*

were also erected at the intersection of Nowomiejska and Podwale Streets. Two iron wells and a sculpture of the Mermaid were set in the Market Place. The whole Market Place was filled with stalls. After the Germans occupied Warsaw in 1915, a group of Polish architects, headed by Kazimierz Skórewicz, acquired the possibility of carrying out inventory work and – in 1917 – of performing slight repairs. After World War One had ended, thorough conservation work was undertaken, aimed at the reconstruction of the former appearance of the interiors and elevations of the Royal Castle.

The work was continued throughout the period between the Wars. Until 1928 it was carried out by the architect Kazimierz Skórewicz, and, later, by the architect Adolf Szyszko-Bohusz. Skórewicz performed most thorough work both inside and outside the Castle. He recovered the interiors of the Vasa chambers and conserved the Stanislaus rooms. He removed pilasters and attic walls from the elevations and restored the former tiled roof. The helmets were also repaired and the Grodzka Tower was covered by a tent roof. In the Castle courtyard, the gothic wall of the Curia Maior, which had survived up to the second floor, was uncovered.

6. *View of the New Town Warsaw by Wojciech Gerson from the second half of the 19th century*

Adolf Szyszko-Bohusz introduced a large number of changes. He changed the roofing from tiles to sheet copper. He removed the roof on the Grodzka Tower, replacing it by a superstructure with a terrace and a balustrade. He demolished the outbuilding at the Grodzka Tower. In the north wing, he introduced a gallery reached by a staircase. At the foot of the Castle he built barracks. At that time a new ferroconcrete construction of the roofs and appropriate protection of the ceilings of the upper storey were made.

In the Old Town, too, work was then begun to recover and restore its former splendour. A large number of houses, after they had been bought by institutions or private persons, were rehabilitated. The town authorities bought three tenements in the north frontage of the Market Place, to house there the Museum of Old Warsaw. Here, renaissance and baroque, coffered and polychromed ceilings of a variety of types were uncovered. In 1928, all the frontages of the Market Place were renovated, and rich coloured decoration was introduced. At that time, the well and the statue of the Mermaid were removed from the Market Place.

In 1936–1938, the defensive walls were uncovered between Nowomiejska Street

13

7. *Fragment of the building of the New Town in Warsaw, according to Władysław Podkowiński, from the end of the 19th century*

and Wąski Dunaj Street. Some part of the walls was preserved at the full height. A previously unknown gothic bridge underneath Nowomiejska Street was also discovered. Greenery, of which the Old Town was in so great need, was introduced in the area between the walls and the moats.

When the September of 1939 came, the invasion of Poland by Nazi Germany soon reached Warsaw. As a result of the siege of the capital, air and artillery shelling, whole districts of the city were destroyed and burned, including a large number of valuable objects of historic interest. The roofs and helmets of the Castle burned, the ceiling over the Ballroom collapsed. The population, the municipal officers and the staff of the National Museum extinguished the fire and salvaged the collections. The shells set on fire the roof of the cathedral, which burned, and the houses in Jezuicka Street. An air-raid bomb demolished the corner house at Wąski Dunaj. After the Germans entered Warsaw in early November, it was decided, as we know from the diary of the Governor Hans Frank, that the Castle should be destroyed and Warsaw would not be rebuilt. Another act of destroying the Castle began.

Its furnishings were taken away, and subsequently a systematic disassembly of the Castle began and charges were set to blow up the Castle. At the time, workers of the National Museum saved from the Castle pieces of the architecture, wainscoting, fireplaces, sculptures etc. For example the whole portal of the Grodzka Gate was salvaged. In this way a large number of details, so essential for the reconstruction of the Castle, were saved. During the 1944 Uprising, Warsaw was destroyed to an enormous extent. The Old Town, under incessant shelling, lay in ruins. The remaining walls of the cathedral and other churches were blown up already after the Uprising. On 27 November, 1944, the walls of the Castle were blown up. The burning out of the city and the demolition of buildings, including a large number of precious objects of historic interest, was consistently and systematically implemented in the whole area of Warsaw, from which all the inhabitants had been removed. The Nazis did not manage to destroy some buildings which were already set to be blown up (e.g. the Grand Theatre, the Łazienki Palace).

The barbarian destruction of the Capital was one of the activities aimed at depriving the Polish nation of the achievements of its culture. The struggle of the Warsaw population to save these achievements continued all through the period of the German occupation. After the liberation, society was definitely determined not only to preserve what remained, but also to give back their former form to the buildings destroyed. The reconstruction of historic buildings in Warsaw, irrespective of their degree of preservation, became an historical, political, emotional and moral necessity. In keeping with the will of the nation and the decision of the authorities of People's Poland, architects – conservators undertook the enormous work of reconstructing whole historic complexes, restoring them with the maximum precision, keeping with reverence each authentic piece, whether preserved in situ or found in the ground. Care was also taken to include these complexes and historic objects into new, contemporary life.

◁ 8. *The Royal Castle in Warsaw – with the Ballroom burning, 17 september, 1939*

◁ 9. *The Royal Castle in Warsaw, the Chinese Cabinet in September 1939*

*10. The Old Town Market Place, Barss Side in 1945*

In this way, the Old and New Towns were rebuilt, and so were the adjacent areas, Krakowskie Przedmieście and Nowy Świat. In this great complex, only the Royal Castle was missing. The necessity of its reconstruction was stated in 1949 by an act of Parliament; however, its implementation, mainly for economic reasons, was postponed. It was finally in January 1971 that it was decided to undertake the reconstruction. The outward form of the Castle complemented with reverence the image of the historically shaped Warsaw, in which the Castle held the meaning of a symbol of the statehood of Poland.

The scope and the range of the reconstruction of the historic objects in Warsaw exceeded the assumptions and postulates of conservation work, bringing into the foreground the question of authenticism of monuments. However, the destruction of Warsaw was not a natural process, but an act of conscious barbarity. Therefore, it is possible to deviate from assumptions which would be respected in any other case. It is in this way that the reconstruction of the historic objects of Warsaw, an expression of the decided will of society and the concentrated effort of those who carried it out, should be understood.

*11. Cathedral in the Old Town in Warsaw in 1945*

# The Reconstruction
# of the Old Town

*Piotr Biegański*

Warsaw, within its mediaeval walls, became the nucleus of the contemporary great agglomeration. The historic districts constitute now an integral part of Greater Warsaw. Thus, the Old Town and the Royal Castle are among the elements of the spatial system of the Capital, and are also objects of national culture, especially cared for by the nation.

At no time in their history have the Old Town and the Royal Castle been subject to such a great catastrophe as during World War Two. The persistence and the premeditation with which the Germans carried out the work of destroying the heart of Warsaw was unprecedented in the history of the civilised world. The programme of a total destruction of everything which could evidence the culture of the Polish nation was beyond human imagination. The state which the Polish authorities met with in Warsaw after its liberation in 1945, presented so tragic an image that only in the bravest minds could the idea of reviving the million-inhabitant city be born.

The decision to rebuild Warsaw and its historic districts was undertaken already in the first days after the liberation. Despite the debris covering the whole Old Town area (at some places, reaching up to the second storeys of houses) and extreme difficulties and risks of moving amidst the cracked and disintegrating walls, in the first rays of the spring sunlight, volunteer teams entered the Old Town, to begin the effort of saving the remains of the historic architecture.

It was soon discovered that, despite the shelling and the burning out of the city, a large number of elements of the architecture of Old Town houses were preserved, and – among the ruins – there were thousands of pieces of their architecture. This fact permitted two simultaneous actions to be undertaken. One consisted in the soonest possible protection of the walls of buildings which survived despite the destruction, the other lay in the recording of relics still among the ruins and in a quest for inventory, archival and iconographic materials, scattered all over the country.

From month to month, and from day to day, this work brought closer the moment when it was possible to begin the project of the reconstruction of the Old Town and the directly adjacent historic districts.

This was no simple task. Even in the first preliminary studies, it appeared that the problems of the rehabilitation of historic complexes must be considered by taking into account contemporary town planning criteria, on which the plans of the reconstruction and expansion of the whole Capital were based. As a consequence of these assumptions, the contemporary town planning problems, transferred to the areas of historic systems, confronted those responsible for the reconstruction of the historic centre with the necessity of solving a large number of such questions, which the conservators of historic objects had not encountered before the War.

Against this background and in the name of the historic truth, long-term and tedious studies were undertaken not only to find out the most correct shape of the Old Town complex, but also to achieve above all such a reconstruction as would, on the one hand, respect all the historical layers of building, and, on the other hand, create the conditions of town planning corresponding to the requirements of contemporary architects.

In this situation, the modern town planning proposals and conservation postulates, resulting from the historical process of the spatial formation of old Warsaw, required analysis and integration.

It followed even from the earliest conceptions of the master plan of Warsaw that the oldest historic districts – the Old and New Towns – were meant to be residential districts, while retaining their tourist significance. This involved the need for considering in the reconstruction programme a large number of modern proposals, which in prewar times had not occurred at all, e.g. the provision of basic services. At the same time, it became obvious that the range of the reconstruction could not be limited to one chosen historical epoch, but, on the contrary, efforts should be made to bring out all the valuable stages which followed in succession, and were the evidence of existential and creative town planning trends in history. Questions thus posed before conservators, architects and planners imposed the obligation of transferring to the next generations not only the most valuable and oldest historic objects, but also those which were evidence of social, political, economic and artistic changes.

The difficult nature of the undertaking, which initially seemed unrealisable, consisted in the lack of practical experience in carrying out a task involving such extensive, specific problems, which was the urban-scale historic monument. Theoretical knowledge, and even the enormous collected archival, iconographic and inventory material, were not sufficient to provide the basis for taking difficult decisions.

It was only inquisitive studies of the preserved buildings or their fragments, carried out systematically over the first years after the end of the war, that permitted a large number of basic doubts to be removed and an elaboration of conservation directives for the reconstruction of the whole Old Town design. They involved not only conservation or technical-construction problems, but above all those upon which it was necessary to make dependent all decisions involved in the planning of the Old and New Towns.

One of the most essential problems in establishing the direction of conservation work was to choose the criteria according to which the actual work was to follow.

WARSOVI

STUDIUM
PERSPEKTYWICZNE
PROYEKTU REKONSTRUKCJI
STAREGO MIASTA
1954

12. A perspective study of the draft design of the reconstruction of the Old Town in Warsaw in 1951

This was particularly the case when in the preserved parts of an object a few historical stages occurred and when each of the stages deserved attention because of its artistic value. For there was hardly anyone who would have thought that beneath the baroque pieces of the elevation plaster in many houses, in many spots, the walls of gothic houses survived and on those walls, in some places, elements of decorative art were preserved in the form of frescoes from the epoch. A detailed inventory carried out after the debris had been removed from the Old Town demonstrated that the mediaeval design of this complex survived to a large extent, for not only magnificent cellars, pieces of elevations, the gable walls of a large number of houses, but also almost the whole mediaeval defensive system, with its towers, crenels, the remains of entrance gates, and also the barbican and the bridge over the moat in front of the former Cracow Gate, were uncovered.

These facts provided the main premise for the decision to base the reconstruction of the Old Town complex on the mediaeval building system, particularly in that this system permitted to the largest extent the postulates of modern planning to be satisfied. It also permitted the elimination of the late 15th-century building inside the Old Town blocks, whose fragments – even if they had not perished under shelling – represented no technical value. As a consequence, in the place of tumbledown houses and heaps of debris, spacious courts, resembling the oldest building forms of the Old Town blocks, appeared.

Studies on the other house walls also revealed a few street-passages forgotten in the 19th century, which – it then appeared – could be restored with no difficulty. The assumption of a gothic plan as the basis for the planning design corresponded thus not only to the conservation postulates, but also involved no difficulty in satisfying the requirements of the modern design of a housing estate.

However, there were other problems in shaping the Old Town district in terms of planning. The question of the third dimension in accepting the idea of the mediaeval plan, the problems of the architectural form of a burgher house, of the street, of the square, and finally of the outline of the whole town appeared to be much more difficult to solve than had at first seemed.

Probably, it would have been most consistent, in keeping with the plan assumed for the Old Town district, to attempt to restore also, within the defensive walls, the gothic character of construction forms and, as a result, a gothic outline of the town. However, neither the number of preserved mediaeval remains, nor iconographic material justified the reconstruction of the Old Town in the gothic convention. What, thus, remained was the possibility of finding the basis in sources and objects dating from the 17th and 18th centuries, i.e. from the period when most Warsaw burghers "modernized" their houses.

In this way, on a mediaeval plan, a new baroque, and partly late renaissance town, arose. New churches appeared, and baroque helmets on towers, which began to dominate the rather uniform type of three-suite building, particularly in the central part of the town.

From the 14th to the early 19th century, the Old Warsaw, together with Castle Square, was surrounded by a single, later a double, ring of defensive walls. A large number of the elements of these walls have survived till the present day, mainly as a result of the fact that they were used in the 18th century as the bearing walls of houses built in the space between the walls and on the site of the former moat. During shelling these walls disintegrated and it was only after the debris had been removed that large parts of fortifications could be uncovered in the original state. This made it possible to include in the historic spatial system of the Old Town yet another, no doubt authentic element, which was a monument of the earliest history of the mediaeval town. It was not easy to establish the conservation and planning criteria, requiring – in addition to thorough knowledge of the history and theory of conservation of monuments – great care and extreme architectural intuition.

It was perhaps made even more difficult to carry out the alternative designs by the continuous complications of intentions brought about by new discoveries and the necessity of solving difficult technical problems, which was the case with the building at 19, Old Town Market Place, where it was only in the middle of masonry work that a brick ceiling was uncovered, which divided the original, two-stores high, gothic cellar. The specific character of the Old Town building and its situation in the centre of the historic system of old Warsaw put the question of its reconstruction among the main problems in the conservation of the Capital at that time.

All the work related to the elaboration of the reconstruction programme and the establishment of the conservation directives was carried out by a team of architects at the Department of Monumental Architecture, the Office of the Reconstruction of the Capital, and after 1947, by the Conservator of Monuments of the capital city of Warsaw. The preliminary work, the initial emergency protection and the professional supervision of the implementation of this great undertaking were performed in four stages. The first stage – through 1947 – involved the collecting of scientific materials, conceptual studies and the provisional emergency protection of those buildings which were to be kept in their original state; the second stage – up to 1950 – included the continued protection, the rebuileling of some objects, the elaboration of a plan for the historic districts the execution of an underground traffic artery, called the W-Z Route, and the making of an initial design of the reconstruction of the Royal Castle.

At that time, its reconstruction was begun by erecting the Grodzka Gate from authentic stone elements and complementing a fragment of the wall of the Castle up to the surviving southwest corner.

In the third stage – up to 1954 – debris was removed from the Old Town area, the uncovered groundfloors and basements of houses were inspected and work was begun on a greater part of the buildings in the Old and New Towns. In the fourth stage – up to 1960 – work was finished on the reconstruction of all the elements of the Old Town complex, including the defensive walls and the surroundings of the historic complex. The subsequent task was to be the reconstruction of the Royal Castle and then Ujazdów Castle as monuments of the patronage of Sigismund III, of the statehood of the Republic and of the capital nature of Warsaw.

The fundamental task of the work thus projected was above all to create in the intended reconstruction of the Old Town as appropriate conditions for the normal course of living in a residential complex as possible, while, at the same time, retaining all the values and the characteristic, features of a historic district. Thus, in addition to the housing function, this district was to cope with tasks resulting from its exceptional cultural and historical role in the new planning conception of Greater Warsaw. Therefore, the problems of the town planning of the whole centre had to be integrated strictly with the conservation postulates, while purely utilitarian questions had to correspond to the possibilities of adapting historic buildings to contemporary life.

Thus, it was necessary to solve two problems of extreme significance in this matter: the problem of preserving the successive stages of the town planning development of the Old Town in terms of current town-making factors, from the Middle Ages to the end of the 18th century, and the problem of up dating the historic building to contemporary requirements, regulations and standards, and of the necessity of equipping it with modern technical installations. It is known that Warsaw owed its economic development not only to its situation on the river, but also to the convenient fords across the Vistula at the routes which intersected at the town. The settlements which arose with the passage of time at the trade routes in areas adjacent to the Old Town became districts of Greater Warsaw. The consequences of such a development of the town, in particular in the south and north, and also on the east and west sides, established the central situation of the Old Town district. However, already in the early 19th century, in the rapidly developing city, this district could no longer satisfy its historical function. At the same time, the character of the old building (mainly of the housing type) in the Old Town area indicated that both the localization and the manner of utilization predestined it to play the role of a housing estate.

Studies carried out from this point of view made the designers certain that in restoring the historic district to life this decision was the correct one. For it created not only the possibilities of the best utilization of the useful space for the needs of housing, but also those of correct localization of services in the estate and of implementing a full cultural and tourist programme, which in the new conditions became an essential element of the utilization of the historic district.

Thus, in the master plan of Warsaw, the localization of the Old Town as a district designed to fulfil housing needs was retained and the conditions were ensured for its existence in the town planning system of a city with a million inhabitants. When preserved and integrated organically into the city organism, the oldest area of the Warsaw spatial system required neither a change in scale, nor an expansion, nor such transformations as would to any degree disturb its historical conception. Even if today the need emerged to site a housing estate on the Vistula escarpment, assuming that the basic spatial system of the city areas on the river were preserved, it would be difficult to find a more convenient and logically justified spot than the Old Town plateau. The direct vicinity of the river and the green areas (on the lower terrace), the convenient situation at the intersecting traffic routes, the good construction conditions – these would all be more than convincing indications that the Old Town could be one of the most attractive residential districts in the centre of a modern city.

The localization of a housing district in the Old Town area involved the necessity of solving the problems of city transportation. As early as the period between the Wars, two routes, perpendicular to each other and linking the south districts with the north ones, and the east with the west, intersected at Castle Square. With the new town planning conception, the streets of the Old Town and the others, directly connected with the former, could not provide good traffic flow without radical changes in the system of streets in this area. It became obvious that traffic would have to be removed from this district, which was reflected in two basic decisions. The first involved the making of a tunnel beneath Castle Square and the historic buildings in its surroundings. The tunnel made it possible to transfer the traffic connecting the east and west districts of the city outside the Old Town complex. The other decision involved rerouting of the north-south traffic through Miodowa Street past Castle Square and the Old Town.

In this way, traffic was practically removed from the whole historical complex, including Castle Square, although the district had until then been at an intersection of transportation routes, and the Old Town housing district (despite its central situation in the capital) was freed from the consequences of transit traffic. Another problem, which resulted from the programme designed for the Old Town district, was the question of adopting the historic houses to a new function. The implementation of intentions in terms of the needs of tourism and of a cultural nature offerred no special difficulties, however, in adapting buildings of the old type for housing purposes serious barriers had to be overcome.

The programmatic assumption postulated distinctly that the groundfloor interiors at the main traffic route Świętojańska Street – Market Place (Kołłątaj Side) – Nowomiejska Street were to house commercial services corresponding to the needs of the district and those related to mass tourism. It agreed in principle with the historic manner of utilizing groundfloors, when the Old Town was the commercial centre of Warsaw and the life of the inhabitants distinctly concentrated at the Old Town Market Place. It was possible, without introducing essential changes in the bearing system of the walls, to house new services and shops and also centres of communal life in the interiors of former craftsmen's workshops and shops. Also, in keeping with the programmatic assumptions, the seats of scientific and cultural institutions could be situated in the Old Town, replacing in some sense the houses of the Old Town patricians, where the cultural life focussed. At the same time,

13. *Building of the Old Town before 1939*

spacious cafes and restaurants arose, in order above all to satisfy the needs of the excursion traffic.

The problem of adapting the burgher house, in turn, used in principle by one owner only, was made complicated by the need of transforming in into a typical set of two or three-room apartments and to suit the requirements of modern technology. Therefore, in the light of the programmatic directives and standards, to be observed in all the newly erected housing estates and not always in agreement with the historical shape of the plan, compromises had to be sought in deviations from both the standards and the former spatial systems of the interiors of particular buildings. In such cases the decision depended on the technical state, the authenticity of the preserved elements and the historic value of the houses under reconstruction.

Thus, in keeping with the conservation assumptions, the original height of storeys of historic houses was maintained and their external outline was reproduced

*14. State of the building of the Old Town after the reconstruction in 1956*

together with the characteristic skylights over the staircases, raised above the roofs. In most cases a typical internal division of houses was reconstructed. However, in damaged buildings, in general, the historic disposition of apartments was not kept, in a tendency to provide standardised living spaces.

An essential and fundamental change with respect to the former installations was the introduction of central heating in the Old Town houses – in addition to the water pipe system and sewerage.

Among the changes which no doubt contributed to the modernization of the Old Town district compared with its state before 1944, one should include the serious transformations of the building inside the blocks. In order to obtain the best hygienic conditions possible in the housing district, the 19th-century building in courtyards was almost fully removed.

Exceptions in the consistent implementation of these principles were only two blocks: one between Świętojańska and Piwna Streets, and another between the

Market Place (Kołłątaj Side) and Piwna Street. In view of the fact, however, that in these blocks not only the groundfloors, but also quite often the first floors were adapted for the purposes of services, only construction elements of no historic significance were demolished. In these two particular cases, historical considerations were given precedence.

In using the whole Old Town complex for housing purposes, much space was also allocated to social institutions and services. Therefore, in proportion to the number of the inhabitants, a creche, a kindergarten, a primary school (outside the ring of the defensive walls), a children's community centre, a social house, a district library, an out-patients' clinic, a chemist's, a post-office and a large number of shops were located in this district. At the same time, in view of the needs of tourism, which was intended as a new element of the function of the historic centre, quite a lot of space was reserved for cafés, restaurants and tourist services, in addition to buildings meant to house museums and the headquarters of social and scientific organizations.

The experiences of many years have demonstrated that the Old Town complex was organized in a correct way, that it ensures good living conditions for its inhabitants, and that this district performs all the functions allocated to it.

In this way, it was possible not only to restore the Old Town to its monumental character, but also to create in the complexes brought back to life an atmosphere in keeping with the criteria of the epochs to which they belonged. The gentle course of the regulation lines, an individualism limited only to the principal heights and bounded by the requirements of the construction law, restrained decorativeness, falling within the canons of current art, finally picturesqueness in toned-down colours, seldom emphasized with gold – they all contributed to the making of a highly humanist mood, corresponding to the Polish psyche.

After more than thirty years, the reconstruction, carried out by the specific Warsaw methods, has been appreciated not only in Poland, but also in the world. Evidence of this can be the evaluations of the inhabitants of the centre, and in particular of those living in the oldest districts of Warsaw, who consider the Old Town authentic and beautiful. Moreover, foreigners connected more closely with the problems of conservation, architecture and town planning, also mention "the Polish operation" of salvaging the remaining authenticity and the "reliable" reconstruction – sparing no praise, pointing out the value of the achievement in artistic and technical terms. Moreover, the success achieved should justly be attributed to the thesis initially proposed, namely that even the oldest complexes can still continue to serve modern needs.

This was made possible by the incessant caution exercised in the specialist supervision by outstanding experts on Polish architecture, who for the first ten years after the war constituted a constant general "staff" (a team evaluating the designs and their execution) of Warsaw conservators, together with well educated designers – architects, the technical services ensuring permanent conservation and

30

15. View of the Old Town, copperplate engraving by Jerzy Miller, from 1960, representing the state before the reconstruction of the Royal Castle

construction supervision and the highly qualified teams of workers devoted whole-heartedly to the memorable task.

In appreciating this heroic and unique evidence of the reverence of the Polish society for the work of past generations and respect for the contribution of the creative conservation thought of our times, the International World Heritage Committee of the UNESCO decided on September 2, 1981, to include the historic centre of Warsaw in the list of the Monuments of the World Heritage.*)

---

*)Patrimoine Culturel de l'humanite les 112 cites inscrits sur la liste du patrimoine mondial – "Centre historique de Varsovie" Bulletin d'Informations 1982, Nr 18, pag. 12–19 (ed. UNESCO)

# The History
# of the Royal Castle
## *Stanisław Lorentz*

At the same time that Warsaw was being built, at the end of the 13th century, in the vicinity of the Town the seat of the Mazovian dukes emerged, founded most probably by Boleslaus II on the high bank of the Vistula, on the ravine in which a stream called Kamionka ran to the river. The duke's stronghold with wooden buildings and earthen-wooden ramparts was a typical defensive design of the times, perfectly suited to the conditions of the terrain. In 1321 historical sources mentioned for the first time the Warsaw Castellan Albert Kuźma. He held his office in the stronghold where, in addition to housing and household buildings, there was a separate shed which functioned as a court-room. In the first half of the 14th century, on the promontory between the ravine and the escarpment of the Vistula, the masonry Great Tower, later called the Broken and Town (Grodzka) Tower, was erected. The former of these later names was probably connected with some catastrophe after which the tower was never rebuilt to its full height. Of the Great Tower, there survive today the foundations of huge granite blocks and a cellar, a dark windowless room, into which prisoners were lowered through a hole in the floor of the groundfloor room. It was a prison up to the first half of the 17th century. As early as the first half of the 14th century, the Great Tower was connected by defensive walls with the municipal fortifications.

In the middle of the 14th century, the castle grounds covered a much greater area, corresponding to the later buildings of the Castle with three courtyards. The front courtyard, called the Apothecary Courtyard, covered much of the present Castle Square. This large fortification circuit housed the duke's residence, court rooms and administration and service buildings. The Castle, which was closely adjacent to the town, was not conceived of as a stronghold overseeing the town, but rather as one of the elements of the municipal system, as the southeast bastion in the town fortifications.

The Warsaw Castle saw great changes under Duke Janusz II, who built in his province masonry castles at Ciechanów, Liw and Czersk. In 1411–1413, on the escarpment at the Great Tower, the splendid, gothic masonry Greater Court (Curia Maior) was erected. It had three storeys, was 47.5 m long, 14.5 m wide and 15 m high, and included a circular tower housing the staircase.

Later on, under the rule of Ladislaus IV, the tower was rebuilt in the baroque style and called the Ladislaus Tower. Even today three basement interiors of the

Greater Court survive, although now restored. The most magnificent of them, 100 m$^2$ in size, has a cross-vaulting, spanned over the vaulting strips, resting on an eight-sided pillar. This most imposing authentic lay gothic interior in Warsaw used probably to house the duke's treasury. It is known from inventories that the treasury included e.g. five gold-fitted mitres, a gilded sword, ducal robes with pearls and precious stones, horse trappings with pearls and sapphires, gilded silver horse saddles, reliquaries, gilded lion's heads, silver table vessels, numerous jewels, furs and expensive textiles. In keeping with the tradition, after the Castle is rebuilt, we intend to use the gothic cellars as the Castle treasury. The groundfloor rooms were used by the Duke's Council and the Duke's Courts, and later by the General Assemblies of the Duchy. The groundfloor also probably housed the Duke's Chancery. Here, the legal acts of the duke were recorded in a book called the Register of the Duchy of Mazovia. On the first floor there were four ducal chambers – three in the Court and one in the Great Tower.

Duke Janusz I the Elder, husband of Anna Danuta, daughter of the Lithuanian duke Kiejstut, was an outstanding ruler. He led his Mazovian troops in the battle of Grunwald, issued numerous statutes, five of which he proclaimed at Warsaw Castle. He took care of the town of Warsaw, granting it a large number of privileges, and in 1426 he provided a magnificent reception for King Ladislaus Jagiełło.

The last two Mazovian dukes kept a sumptuous and imposing court at the Castle. They died young – Stanislaus in 1524, Janusz III in 1526. Their sister, Ann, endowed for them at St John's church a renaissance tombstone of red marble. King Sigismund the Old came to Warsaw Castle. In 1529 the Duchy of Mazovia became part of the Crown territory and the King held in Warsaw the first General Parliament of the Crown.

From 1564, King Sigismund Augustus frequently stayed in Warsaw, where, after the Union of Lublin, the parliament sessions were moved. In 1570, the General Parliament of the whole Commonwealth was held here. The new functions of Warsaw required an essential reconstruction and expansion of the Castle. Work on it began in 1596, supervised by two outstanding renaissance architects: Giovanni Battista Quadro, known for his reconstruction of the town hall in Poznań, and Giacomo Perro, who worked on the reconstruction of the Silesian castle in Brzeg. The King's death in 1572 interrupted the work at the Warsaw Castle, although a great deal had been done over the three years. The Greater Court had been thoroughly rebuilt, where on the groundfloor a suite of three halls, with one, two and three pillars, arose. These halls had survived until the destruction of the Castle and have now been reconstructed. The room with three pillars was the Delegates' Chamber, over it, on the first floor, was the Senate Chamber, the main Parliament Chamber. Thus, the edifice of the Duke's Council and the Mazovian Parliament was adapted to the needs of the General Assembly of the Commonwealth, which held sessions here till the reign of the Saxon dynasty.

As an expansion of the Greater Court, a two-storeyed, cellared royal residential building was erected. It was situated along the escarpment, at an obtuse angle to the former building, thus determining the later five-sided shape of the main courtyard. A separate tower contained a staircase. In the great chamber a music gallery was built. The royal chambers were splendidly furnished, the ceilings were painted, and on the walls Arras tapestries from the famous Jagiellonian collection hung. The Smaller Court, where the Princess Ann lived, was also rebuilt and modernized. The music edifice and the house of Jurko Klaryka or Jerzy Jasińczyk, the conductor of the royal choir, indicated the artistic predilection of the royal family. The new seat of the King was connected by a gallery with the rooms of the Princess, from where another porch led to St John's church. Work was begun on a permanent bridge across the Vistula.

During the interregnum, in January 1573, a convocation session of the Parliament, preceding the election, was held. It was then that a significant act, called the Warsaw Confederation, a commendable event in Polish history, was passed. The act ensured peace between the Catholics and believers of other persuasions, political emancipation, freedom of conscience and mutual tolerance. At the election session of the Parliament in April and May, 1573, the principles of the political system of the Commonwealth were established in an act, called the Henry Articles, which was then confirmed by Henri Valois. The subsequent rulers had to pledge to observe this act.

On February 25, 1578, King Stephen Bathory received Duke Georg Frederick who came from Prussia to pay a vassal's homage. In the Commonwealth the Castle played an increasingly significant role as the seat of the legislative authorities and an important royal residence.

The process of transferring the main centre of power in the Commonwealth from Cracow to Warsaw, which had been initiated by Sigismund Augustus, was taken over by King Sigismund III Vasa after he came to the throne in 1587. In this connection, from 1598, the Castle complex was expanded, acquiring in its general outline the shape it would have until 1939. The construction took 20 years, up to 1619, but even later the interior decoration continued. The gothic Great or Town (Grodzka) Tower, the Greater Court and the residence of Sigismund Augustus were kept, while the north, west and south wings were added; the whole enclosed a five-sided courtyard. The new wings had three storeys. From the south the courtyard could be entered through the Great (Grodzka) Gate; from the north, through the Senators' Gate; from the west, i.e. from the side of the town, through the Nobility Gate in a 60 m tower topped with a tall helmet, called the Sigismund Tower or the Clock Tower, because of the great clock set in it in 1622. The Sigismund Tower dominated the whole Castle complex and in the view of the Castle in the period between the Wars it was a particularly characteristic accent, connected with the Column of Sigismund III. On both ends of the elevation, about 90 m long, small towers were set, which emphasized the corners of the five-sided

*16. Homage paid to Sigismund III by the Shuyski Tsars at the Parliament in 1611, copperplate by Tomasz Makowski, according to a painting by Tomasso Dolabella*

courtyard. These small towers were removed during the reconstruction of the Castle under the rule of Augustus III, in the middle of the 18th century.

It can be supposed that the expansion of the Castle was designed, or at least approved, by the royal architect Giovanni Battista Trevano, who worked at Wawel during the reign of Sigismund III.

The construction was the work of Giacomo Rotondo and later, after 1614, that of Matteo Castelli; the sculpture in stone and marble was executed by Paolo di Corte.

In 1611 the King made his permanent residence at the Castle and the supreme administration moved here from Cracow; therefore, the residence must have been finished for the most part at that date. When in the autumn of 1620. Michał Piekarski attempted to assassinate the King, who went on Sundays and feasts, with his family and court, to hear mass, it was decided to provide a covered passage between the Castle and the church. A corridor, i.e. a gallery 80 m long, was built through the buildings of the kitchen courtyard. This corridor has survived up to the present day; there is a fragment of it at the gate giving access from the kitchen

35

courtyard to Kanonia Street. The main outline of the Castle was monumental, characterized by simplicity and cubicity, typical of the period style of Polish architecture in the first half of the 17th century in Poland, called the "Vasa style". In turn, the interiors, which corresponded stylistically to the Roman architecture in the transitional period between mannerism and baroque, had splendid decoration.

The Great Senatorial Hall, where the Shuyski Tsars, brought as prisoners by the Hetman Stanisław Żółkiewski, paid homage to Sigismund III, had a coffered ceiling with richly painted beams with suspended rosettes. In the first and second antechambers there were two ceiling paintings by Tomasso Dolabella, representing the conquest of Smoleńsk and exactly the homage paid by the Tsars to Sigismund III. The Tsar Peter I took the two paintings away from the Warsaw Castle in 1707. On the walls tapestries hung. A week after the homage of the Tsars, the Elector of Brandenburg Johannes Sigismund Hohenzollern came to Warsaw to pay homage to the King as the Regent of Royal Prussia. Since crowds wished to witness this ceremony, it was decided that it would be held in Krakowskie Przedmieście Street, in front of the Bernardine church, for the Senators' Hall could not accommodate so many spectators and the construction work in the Castle courtyard was not finished. The last Prussian homage, paid in 1641 by the Duke Frederick Wilhelm, later called the Grand Elector, to Ladislaus IV, was held in the Senators' Hall.

Particular fame was gained by the Marble Cabinet, fitted out after 1619 and considered the most beautiful chamber of the Castle. The multi-coloured marbles to face the walls were brought from Flanders; the ceiling painting, executed by Dolabella, represented the coronation of Sigismund III; another painting placed here showed the Austrian Archduke Maximilian being taken prisoner by Jan Zamoyski in the battle of Byczyna in 1588. This Cabinet, which had under the rule of Ladislaus IV been decorated with portraits of Polish kings, was reproduced in changed form at the time of Stanislaus Augustus Poniatowski.

In the reign of the King Ladislaus IV, the tower with a staircase, situated in the bend of the elevation of the east wing, acquired a baroque shape and helmet, designed probably by the architect Constantino Tencalla. In the north part of this wing, i.e. just as under the rule of Sigismund Augustus and later, up to the times of the Saxon dynasty, there were the royal dwelling apartments. The Castle housed the central state offices: of the marshall, of the chancellor and of the treasurer; thus, the Royal Castle in Warsaw was the royal residence and at the same time the seat of the legislative power and the supreme executive administration. In 1621, at the foot of the Vistula escarpment, a defensive wall with two strong bastions was erected. In 1638–1643, at the north bastion, a small palace was built for Charles Ferdinand Vasa, brother of Ladislaus IV, designed by the royal architect Giovanni Battista Ghisleni. This palace, known from views of Warsaw from the Vistula, was destroyed by the Swedes in 1656.

The monument of Sigismund III, erected in 1643 by his son, Ladislaus IV, was an object most closely connected with the Castle. It was designed by Tencalla, the figure of the King was sculpted by Clemente Molli and cast by Daniel Tym. The Column of Sigismund became a characteristic Warsaw motif, strongly integrated with views of the Castle from the side of Krakowskie Przedmieście and the Old Town, in particular when at the beginning of the 19th century, in place of the former buildings of the front courtyard, Castle Square arose. Under Vasa rule, Warsaw was not only the political and administrative capital, but also became the main centre of science, art and culture, to which, in addition to the royal patronage, that of the magnates also contributed. On the occasion of court ceremonies, e.g. the weddings of Ladislaus IV and the Emperor's daughter Cecilia Renata, of John Casimir and Mary Louise Gonzaga, or of the Princess Ann Catherine and the Elector Palatine Philip Wilhelm, splendid receptions with dancing and entertainments were held at the Castle. The royal apartments were filled with works of art. Sigismund III mainly imported paintings from Italy; Ladislaus IV, from the Low Countries, including a large number of paintings by Rubens; John Casimir also had works by Rembrandt. A significant role in the decoration of the Castle interiors was played by artistic tapestry – arrases and Eastern carpets.

In the Vasa period the theatre reached a very high level. At the time of Sigismund III, troupes of English comedians performed at the Castle. Even during Shakespeare's lifetime and soon after his death, *Romeo and Juliet*, *The Merchant of Venice*, *King Lear* and *Hamlet* were staged in the theatre. The King's orchestra had 60 players. Ladislaus IV established at the Castle a permanent opera theatre, where professional actors performed. It was then that a special theatre hall was built in the south wing, equipped with the most modern technical equipment, including a trapdoor and a system of lines permitting changes in the decoration. The plastic design and the baroque effect were received most enthusiastically.

In the field of science, royal patronage was universal and modern: Ladislaus IV corresponded with Galileo, brought telescopes and other technical devices from Italy, Mary Louise bought in France equipment for scientific studies and created the Physical Cabinet at the Castle. Lively contacts were maintained with scholars from various countries.

The flourishing scientific and artistic life at the Castle and the Warsaw magnate courts was stopped in 1655 by the Swedish invasion. Although the Royal Castle was not demolished or burnt, its interiors were vandalized and looted. All the precious things at the Castle were either taken away to Sweden or destroyed. Even today, Swedish collections include numerous works of art, objects of historic interest and all kinds of cultural goods, brought from Poland during the Swedish invasions in the 17th century and the early 18th century – including a large number of objects from the Royal Castle. Although in the second half of the 17th century the Castle was utilized, parliamentary sessions were held, kings lived here, but they neither undertook its thorough reconstruction nor took proper care of its equipment. One should note, however, that in 1662, in the surviving Theatre Hall, *Le Cid* by Corneille, translated by Morsztyn, was staged, and under the rule of

Sobieski various shows, ballet performances, productions of French and Italian comedies were performed, and in 1694, on the occasion of the marriage of the Princess Teresa Kunegunda, an Italian troupe gave a performance of an opera by Lampugnani.

Under the Saxon dynasty the Castle saw great changes. Early in the reign of Augustus II, before 1704, the Delegates' Hall was moved from the groundfloor of the Greater Court to the first floor of the southwest corner, on the side of the Column of Sigismund III. This single-storey room served as the Delegates' Chamber until the November Uprising. The Senate Hall was first rebuilt and, after 1735, moved to the north-west corner, on the side of Świętojańska Street. The interior was designed by the architect Joachim D. Jauch. The room with pairs of Corinthian pilasters on the walls was decorated with huge emblems of Poland and the Grand Duchy of Lithuania and the coats of arms of the districts. The walls and the floor were covered with red cloth. The throne and some architectural and decorative elements were taken from the former Senate Hall. It was in the new hall, whose architecture had not undergone any large changes by the end of the 18th century, that the Third of May Constitution was passed. Still another change was made by making a separate Throne Hall in one of the royal living rooms, remaining in their former place in the southeast wing.

At first, Augustus planned a great expansion of the Castle but the militarily turbulent times made him abandon these intentions; anyway, the King's interest turned later in another direction and the Saxon Palace became his real residence. Work on a greater scale was undertaken in the reign of Augustus III, when the plans foresaw an expansion of the northeast wing and the erection of a monumental façade on the Vistula side. It was demanded that the design should be practical, taking into account the conditions of the terrain and expense. The conception of such a façade was elaborated by the architect Gaetano Chiaveri before 1737. This design, modified by the Saxon architects, was approved by the King and in 1741–1746 the construction work was executed under the supervision of Antoni Solari.

The picturesque rococo façade on the escarpment became one of the dominating effects in the panorama of the town. Recorded in the Panorama of Warsaw by Canaletto, it would later be painted and drawn by numerous artists, until the present day. The façade had three projections: the great central one where the Audience Hall was planned (at the time of Stanislaus Augustus the Ballroom was fitted out here) and two side ones. The south projection contained the King's Bedroom (the Throne Hall in the reign of Stanislaus Augustus), while the north projection housed a chapel. On the ground-floor storey the projections were linked by four-arcaded galleries on which the balconies of the first floor rested. The roof over the central projection, containing the two-storeyed Audience Hall, was of the mansard type with an attic wall, on which a large sculpted cartouche with the coats of arms of the Commonwealth and the King were set. At the sides were allegorical statues. In the triangular frontals over the side projections, in rich sculpted decoration, there were shields with the crowned initials of the King, carried by winged female figures – the allegories of Fame. These works were carried out by Jan Jerzy Plersch, one of the most outstanding Warsaw sculptors in the rococo period.

Since in expanding the Castle the former service buildings were eliminated from the kitchen courtyard, it was necessary to locate the service and auxiliary interiors elsewhere. Therefore, in 1748–1750, at the foot of the escarpment on the Vistula, the Great Outbuilding, 195 m long, was erected. It was a single-storey building, containing the apartments of the court service and storerooms. On the ground floor, the façade of the outbuilding was divided by 36 blank arcades. Its inhabitants reached the Castle through two covered wooden galleries. The Great Outbuilding can perfectly be seen in the Panorama of Warsaw by Canaletto from 1770. In the early 19th century it was covered by Kubicki's great arcaded terrace, behind which the remains of an 18th century building have survived up to date.

When after the death of Augustus III, in September 1763, an inspection of the edifice of the Castle and its interiors was carried out, it appeared that they were quite neglected. The inspection record said that *its state shows the bareness of the rooms on the principal floor, quite becoming in part of the wing on the side of the Vistula, good for incidental residence only, in the other wings the passages themselves and the ordinary rooms partly in ruin, the same on the second floor, while the groundfloor contained almost solely vaulted rooms, apart from some used as offices and archives... the baseness of the other rooms is indicated by its dwellers of the lowest service only who were then there.* In this state the Castle was not a fit royal residence.

When it became obvious in March 1764 that Stanislaus Augustus Poniatowski would be elected King, it appeared to be necessary to undertake steps towards the most rapid possible preparation of the Castle for the seat of the new ruler, who had no other residence in Warsaw (the Saxon kings had a palace of their own). Therefore, the Convocation Parliament decided that the work should be continued. In the reign of Augustus III it had dragged for years causing the Castle interiors to become unusable. For example the architect Jakub Fontana had for a long time been rebuilding the Delegates' Hall. He was also commissioned with the execution of the act of parliament. As early as March 1764, Stanislaus Augustus Poniatowski sent the Warsaw merchant Czempiński to carry out purchases and orders for the Castle. Stanislaus Augustus' care of the appearance of the Castle resulted not only from the utilitarian needs but also from his artistic predilections and suggested the future royal patronage, which would be so significant for the Polish culture. Stanislaus Augustus was a very versatile man, he was interested in ancient and Italian arts, in the literature and the political system of England, in the theatre, however, from his young years he was most closely connected with French culture.

In the spring of 1765, the painter-decorator Jean Pillement came, to execute at the Royal Castle wall decorations in the rococo style, with Chinese motifs – and to leave Warsaw after a few years' stay, perhaps because the style of his works no longer satisfied the changed artistic taste. In the summer of 1765, the architect Victor Louis, who would later enjoy great fame in France, paid a short visit. He was only to become acquainted with the Castle edifice and its surroundings and with the taste and wishes of the King, and later, in Paris, to design the reconstruction of the palace. In 1786, the sculptor André Le Brun came to Warsaw. The most urgent task was to decorate the King's living rooms, and therefore this was the first work to be undertaken. As early as the end of August 1764 the first transports came from Rouen via Gdańsk, by land and sea. The wall hangings were bought by Czempiński in Lyon. Their inventory permits some knowledge of the appearance of a few Castle rooms in the early years of the King Stanislaus Augustus' rule. Damask in three colours: crimson, green and white was ordered for the Audience Hall; crimson, white and pink damask, prepared earlier for one of the apartments of the French King Louis XV, was for the Bedroom, lampas with Chinese figures and flowers was for the Knights' Hall; crimson and white damask with a golden border was for the Dining Room; fabric painted with small branches and flowers was for the Study; and white and yellow hangings, bought in Germany, were for the Council Chamber. Furniture, mirrors and works by the goldsmith François Thomas

40

Germani, clocks, mantelpiece vases, chandeliers and other decorative objects, were also sent from Paris.

These objects were executed in the neoclassical style, already current in those years and called the style of Louis Seize.

Just as in the early reign of Augustus II, so now great, fantastic designs for the reconstruction of the Castle and a transformation of its surroundings were developed. The first design was made by Fontana in 1764, the successive ones were the work of Louis in 1766. A few dozens of Louis's water colour plates survive in the Cabinet of Prints of the University Library in Warsaw. In fact only a few of Louis's designs were implemented, and even those would be transformed in the later rebuilding of the Castle interiors in the reign of Stanislaus Augustus; nevertheless the complex of Louis's designs itself was a valuable contribution to the history of the development of architectural thought, not only in Poland, but also in France. In his later interior designs, Fontana, until his death in 1773, would take into account Louis's conceptions.

Stanislaus Augustus intended to build a monumental complex of Parliament Halls: the Delegates' and Senators' Halls. It was proposed that they should be located close to each other in the northwest corner of the Castle, on the side of Świętojańska Street and in the kitchen courtyard. The Senate Hall was to be covered with a dome and splendidly decorated with columns and sculptures. The design of the decoration of the great Theatre Hall, the Painting Gallery and the Library reflected the ideas of the Age of Enlightenment and the personal predilection of the King. The Castle was to be separated from the town by demolishing the buildings in the front courtyard. It was designed, in various versions, that just where now Castle Square is, there should be a reception square enclosed by colonnades; it was also intended that the whole architectural-town planning complex, including the cathedral, should be transformed. Louis went as far as to strike a great avenue to the west, through the Old Town. In later years, the architect Efraim Szreger elaborated a programme of the Castle complex towards Krakowskie Przedmieście Street. He proposed that a column of John III Sobieski should be erected as a counterpart to the Column of Sigismund III, and in the centre of the square, in the opening of the Triumphal Arch, he envisaged an equestrian statue of Stanislaus Augustus Poniatowski.

In the designs by the architect Domenico Merlini, who followed Fontana, different versions were elaborated. One involved new great wings of the Castle with colonnades, projected towards Krakowskie Przedmieście Street, in others he demolished part of the west wing, created a great square in front of the Castle and proposed that the same tower as the Sigismund Tower should be set on the other side of the square. Great terraces and monumental stairways to the Vistula were to be made, however, it all ended in a much more modest solution. A boulevard was built on the Vistula, with a road 10 m wide, on it. It was only in the early 19th century that a conception proposed by Louis as early as 1766 – to create a great picturesque base of the solid of the Castle in the panorama of the town from across the Vistula – was undertaken anew and carried out.

From the water colour plates, it is possible to discern the character that the interiors of the rooms executed to Louis's designs had and what was taken over from him. For example in a plate with a design of the Throne Hall, in the decoration of the door wings, the motif of crossed banners, sculpted in wood and gilded, can be seen – an analogous motif will later be encountered on the doors of the great Ballroom; the ornament of the King's initials in a laurel wreath is frequently repeated; the wings of the doors of the magnificent King's Bedroom are decorated with crossed laurel branches – they would later be found on the doors of the new Throne Hall.

In the framework of Louis's designs, the sculptor-decorator Jean Louis Prieur designed bronze objects and other artistic products. He sent to the King a few dozen water colour designs, representing e.g. clocks, sconces, candlesticks, chandeliers etc. They corresponded perfectly to Louis's designs, and the fact that at least some of them were executed is evidenced by a few of the surviving Castle bronze objects, e.g. the candlesticks with eagles in the Throne Hall or the appliqué work in the Ballroom.

On 15 March, 1767 a fire broke out in the south wing of the Castle. This unexpected event necessitated an immediate reconstruction of this part of the edifice. In 1768, between the Town Gate and the Town Tower, Jakub Fontana rebuilt, in the early neoclassical style, the staircase, the Mier Guard Hall and the Guard Officers' Hall. The walls of the staircase were divided by sets of stone Ionic pilasters and decorated with stuccowork. The walls of the Mier Hall (from the name of Józef Mier, the commander of the King's personal guard, who were on duty here) were articulated by Corinthian pilasters between which garlands hung. In the stucco decoration, there were puttoes among panoplies, laurel branches and flowers.

In 1768, Fontana commenced a complete reconstruction of the Marble Study, which had been built at the time of Sigismund III; in the reign of Ladislaus IV it had been decorated with portraits of Polish kings, however, due to neglect in later years it fell into disrepair. Stanislaus Augustus decided to restore the work of his predecessors and, while retaining the original idea, to give it a new shape. The interior decoration was designed by Fontana. The walls were faced with multicolour marble. At the top, over the cornice of the doors, there ran a frieze on which 22, oval and rectangular portraits of Polish kings, painted by Bacciarelli, were set. Over the fireplace there was a great full-size portrait of Stanislaus Augustus in coronation robes. The ceiling painting by Bacciarelli represented *Fame proclaiming the acts of Polish monarchs.*

The cartouche with the coats of arms of Poland, Lithuania and the King, topped with a golden crown and supported by the allegorical female figures of Peace and Justice, was sculpted by Le Brun in marble. The Marble Cabinet was finished in 1771, while its opening was commemorated by Adam Naruszewicz with his poem

18. Senators' Hall at the Castle during the passing of the Third of May Constitution, 1791. Etching by Józef Łęski, according to a drawing by Jean Pierre Norblin

On the Marble Room Newly Decorated with Portraits of Polish Kings at the Order of His Majesty King Stanislaus Augustus. An Ode on the Anniversary of the Election of His Royal Majesty Presented to Him in the Year MDCCLXXI. The appearance of the Marble Cabinet was recorded in five water colours executed with complete perfection by the architect Jan Chrystian Kamsetzer. Since all the essential elements of the Cabinet – paintings, sculptures, even a console-table and a clock – survived, Kamsetzer's water colours permit a strict reconstruction of its architecture, including the equipment. With his cycle of kings' portraits Bacciarelli had preceded by a more than a hundred years the well known cycle by Matejko. Two hundred years ago the Royal Castle was the scene of events of permanent significance in the history of Poland. At the beginning of the rule of Stanislaus Augustus Poniatowski, Andrzej Zamoyski justified at the Castle the programme of his political group: *It is not sufficient to establish goverments, to establish laws – it is also necessary to form people so that they could love and defend the fatherland, establish laws and be obedient.* The debates at the Castle gave birth to the idea of

43

establishing the Knights' School. Here, at the Partition Parliament in 1773, the protesting Nowogród delegate, Tadeusz Rejtan, wishing to stop the conciliatory delegates, fell at the threshold of the Delegates' Hall and cried stretching his arms: *Kill me, tread on me, but do not kill the fatherland!* Before the War a painting by Matejko, representing Rejtan, was at the Castle. It is now exhibited at the National Museum in Warsaw and will return to the Castle. On 14 September, 1773, at the Castle, the Parliament passed an act establishing the Commission on National Education of the Polish Crown and the Grand Duchy of Lithuania – the first secular state education authority in the world. An expression of the cultural patronage of the King were the socalled Thursday Suppers which were held at the Castle or sometimes at the Palace-on-the-Island at Łazienki.

Between 1774 and 1785, when Domenico Merlini was the main royal architect, beautiful royal living and reception apartments were constructed. Just as the earlier rooms by Fontana, just as the Royal Łazienki, they represented the Polish version of the neoclassical style, justly called the "Stanislaus Augustus style", for the personal taste of the King significantly affected the work of artists. All that was made then was a result of the common efforts of architects, sculptors, painters and decorators. The artistic achievements of the Age of Enlightenment constituted a praiseworthy chapter in the history of Polish art.

In 1774–1777 Merlini executed the Canaletto Hall, the Chapel, the Former Audience Hall, the King's Bedroom, the Dressing Room and the Cabinet. The quite modest architecture in the Canaletto Hall was only to play the function of a framework for a set of views of Warsaw, painted by Bernardo Bellotto, called Canaletto. The walls were densely covered by 22 views of Warsaw, painted in 1770–1780, representing the streets and squares of the town and Wilanów. For the subject of his works, Canaletto chose the busiest arteries of the then centre – e.g. Krakowskie Przedmieście Street and Miodowa Street. His most magnificent painting was the great panorama made in 1770, with a view of the town and the Castle in the centre. In the Hall, there was also a painting by Canaletto representing the election of Stanislaus Augustus. Fortunately, all these works have survived.

In the Town Tower, next to the Canaletto Hall, the King's Chapel was fitted out. Eight green, Corinthian stucco columns supported the coffered dome with a hundred and twenty rosettes. The columns, together with their capitals, were removed, and thus salvaged, before the destruction of the Castle. The Canaletto Hall communicated in the suite on the side of the River with the Former Audience Hall, so called because it had for a long time been the throne room of Stanislaus Augustus. A beautiful, round ceiling painting by Bacciarelli, glorifying Geography, Painting, Trade, Woodcarving and Agriculture, with a figure of the Polish Genius and that of Peace, indicated the development of science, art and the economy in the reign of Stanislaus Augustus. A counterpart to the round ceiling painting was the beautiful pavement, composed in a circle of multi-coloured wood. The walls were dressed with amaranth damask, in the overdoors there were paintings by Bacciarel-

*19. View of the Castle from Krakowskie Przedmieście Street in the 19th century, according to Jan Seydlitz*

li, representing the allegories of Bravery, Wisdom, Religion and Justice. Bacciarelli's paintings, furniture and objects of the artistic industry were saved.

Next to the Former Audience Hall, also in the suite on the side of the Vistula, there was the King's Bedroom. Its original appearance was recorded in Bacciarelli's painting *Stanislaus Augustus Receives a Miller*; it is a scene where the King receives in his Bedroom at the Castle a miller from Marymont and his wife, who gave him shelter when on 3 November, 1771, he was kidnapped by the Bar Confederates. Beside the King, who lies wounded, the painting shows doctors and persons from his family and entourage, including Bacciarelli himself. After Merlini's reconstruction, the appearance of the Bedroom changed. The walls were faced with wainscoting of yew-wood, enclosing straw-coloured satin. Two over-doors by Bacciarelli were saved.

In the adjacent King's Dressing Room, in 1927, was set a beautiful antique marble copy of Praxiteles's sculpture *Resting Satyr*. At present the sculpture is at the National Museum in Warsaw. Next to the Dressing Room there was the King's Study, also called the King's Chancery. In the earliest years of the reign of Stanislaus Augustus, this room was decorated with wall paintings by Pillement, representing Chinese scenes. In the period of the Duchy of Warsaw, arabesque paintings were executed on the walls, to decorate this interior until the last war.

The great façade on the side of the Vistula, from the middle of the 18th century, hid five rooms. In the south projection there was the Throne Hall, one of the most beautiful rooms in the Castle. Its walls were faced with sculpted and gilded wainscoting, enclosing fields dressed with red damask and filled with mirrors. Inside the room, facing the windows, the King's throne stood. The throne chair with the coats of arms of the Commonwealth and the King stood under a canopy, whose background and sky were decorated with silver embroidered eagles. It was those eagles that on 10 October, 1939, Hans Frank himself tore out and presented to the Nazi dignitaries from his entourage.

On the mantelpiece were set four marble copies of antique sculptures, made in Rome in 1785–1786, representing Caesar, Hannibal, Scipio and Pompey. 18th-century console-tables with Italian-made mosaic plates were set beside the throne before the last war. Glass cases on those tables contained the coronation sword of Stanislaus Augustus, his coronation sceptre and the chain of the Order of the White Eagle. From the Throne Hall, all the objects mentioned above, and also bronze candlesticks with eagles, the wings of doors ornated by interwoven laurel branches, large pieces of richly sculpted and gilded wainscoting and decorative elements, were salvaged.

Next to the Throne Hall there was the small eight-sided Conference Closet. In it, Jan Bogumił Plersch painted arabesque-grotesque decoration on a golden background, amidst which six portraits of rulers contemporary with Stanislaus Augustus were hung: Louis Seize, George III, Catherine II, Josef II, Frederick II, Pope Pius VI and the King of Sweden, Gustavus III – the last by the known Swedish painter, Per Krafft. In the Closet there was a round-top table of Sèvres china dating from 1777. All these objects were salvaged, including even the wall paintings by Plersch, which were cut off the walls and moved in pieces to the National Museum.

Adjacent to the Throne Hall was the Knights' Hall, one of the most imposing rooms at the Castle. It was – just as the Marble Cabinet and the Conference Closet were – an expression of historicism, which was simultaneously strong in the works by Adam Naruszewicz, which arose on the initiative and with the support of the King. The walls of the Hall were filled with six great history paintings by Bacciarelli, namely: *Casimir the Great Listens to the Pleas of Peasants*, *Ladislaus Jagiełło Grants Privileges to the Cracow Academy*, *Prussian Homage*, *Union of Lublin*, *Chocim Treaty* and *John Sobieski at Vienna*. In the overdoors there were portraits of famous Poles, including Copernicus, painted by Bacciarelli. The gallery of eminent Poles was complemented with a series of twenty two bronze portraits of statesmen, leaders, scientists and poets, the work of the sculptors Le Brun and Giacomo Monaldi. The large four busts represented Jan Zamoyski, Paweł Sapieha, Stefan Czarniecki and Stanisław Jabłonowski. The marble statue of Fame by Le Brun and the marble figure of Chronos by Monaldi, where Chronos pointed with the blade of the scythe at the hours on a band encircling the globe of a starry sky, were related to the themes to which the Hall was devoted. The whole equipment of the Hall and a large number of architectural and sculpted details were salvaged.

The Ballroom was the last of the great reception halls at the Castle. Its interior was surrounded by pairs of Corinthian columns of golden stucco. In the doorway recess, in an overdoor, there was a marble medalion with a profile portrait of the King, surrounded by figures, also of white marble, representing Justice and Peace. By the walls on both sides, there were two marble statues, of Stanislaus Augustus as Apollo, with a lyre and a laurel wreath, and of Catherine II as Minerva. All these sculptures, the work of Le Brun, and also the door wings, candlesticks, appliqué work and a large number of details were salvaged. Unfortunately, the great ceiling painting by Bacciarelli, 150 m² large, representing *The Division of the Four Elements, or Jupiter Brings the World out of Chaos*, burned down on 17 September, 1939. However, in addition to a photograph, these are also large colour oil designs painted by Bacciarelli, which can help reconstruct the ceiling painting.

The Dining Hall, also called the Council Room, where the Thursday Suppers were held, had no special architectural decoration. Between the Wars, there were four paintings by French artists, which were ordered by the King in Paris and brought in 1768. In scenes from ancient history, they represented the ideas of generosity, justice, competition and agreement. *Scipio's Moderation* was the work of Joseph Maria Vien.

The last of the rooms in the suite of the great apartments was called the Saxon Chapel, for such was its function. In the times of Stanislaus Augustus it served as a concert and theatre hall.

The Palace Under the Tin Roof was purchased and integrated with the Castle complex in 1776.

The King's Library was in a separate wing, erected in 1779–1782 by Merlini. The Library, 56 m long, divided by two pairs of Ionic columns into three parts, is decorated by stucco medalions, symbolizing the fields of science and art represented in the King's book collection. This room was not destroyed and has now been rehabilitated.

In the last years of the rule of Stanislaus Augustus the Castle saw extremely important events. During the Four-Year Parliament, demonstrating burghers came to the Parliament in the "Black Procession" and gained their rights. On 3 May, 1791, in the Senate Hall, the Constitution was passed. From there, they went to St John's church to swear allegiance to it. This event was showed by Matejko in a painting, which was to be set in the Parliament Hall at the Castle after independence was regained. The will of Matejko will be fulfilled. The act of the passing of the Constitution was recorded by contemporary artists in drawings and engravings, and in a large oil painting by the painter Kazimierz Wojniakowski. It was very significant that in the drawings and paintings the King could hardly be seen in the far ground; the artists were interested in the crowd, the human mass, all the estates, mediators, delegates and senators, and only then, among them, the King, thus, giving convincing evidence that the passing of the Constitution was considered to be an all-national act.

After the third partition the Castle became empty. At that time it was commented on a large number of entries in the inventory: "Gone with the Prussians". When, in December 1806 and January 1807, Napoleon lived at the Castle, the furniture for the apartment chosen for him had to be borrowed from private palaces. After the Duchy of Warsaw was established the Castle became the residence of the Saxon king and the Warsaw Duke Frederick Augustus. At that time slight modifications were made, e.g. the walls of the rooms on the side of the courtyard, beside the Throne Hall, called the Yellow and Green Rooms, where Stanislaus Augustus had his dinning room, were decorated with arabesque paintings.

*20. View of the Castle from the Pancer viaduct before 1939*

After Congress Poland was established in 1815, both of the Parliament Halls were renovated and their interiors modernized. At the order of the Grand Duke Constantine, the former Saxon Chapel was turned into an Orthodox Chapel. In this chapel, in 1820, the Grand Duke married Joanna Grudzińska. In 1817 and 1818 the buildings in the front courtyard and the former Cracow Gate were pulled down. In front of the façade with the Sigismund Tower, Castle Square arose. Thus, the intentions of the King and the Stanislaus architects were implemented, however, only in terms of the demolition, without attempting to shape Castle Square according to designs by the architect Jakub Kubicki. Kubicki also carried out another proposal which had been put forth for a long time – namely, in 1818–1820, he made a large arcaded terrace with a stairway at the edge of the Vistula escarpment. At the foot of the Castle, on the Vistula, a park was laid out, which in 1856 was reworked to serve as exercise ground and barracks for the personal guard of the Emperor's governor, later for those of the Russian governors – general.

On 25 January 1831, when the people demonstrated in support of the Decembrists in Castle Square, in the Delegates' Chamber at the Castle, Nicholas I was deposed as the Polish king. On 2 April, 1831, the prisoners and banners taken at the battles of Wawer and Dębe Wielkie were brought to Warsaw. Five Russian banners were solemnly deposited at the Castle.

After the fall of the November Uprising, a bitter enemy of Poland, the Field Marshall Ivan Paskevich, took up residence at the Castle. He began a systematic devastation of the Castle. In 1832 Canaletto's paintings were taken away to Petersburg, and in 1833, at the order of Paskevich, marbles with portraits of Polish kings were torn off the walls of the Closet. At the order of Paskevich, too, the Senate Hall, memorable for the passing of the Third of May Constitution, was divided into two storeys and apartments were fitted out here for Russian clerks, while the Delegates' Hall was transformed into offices. In the middle of the 19th century, the elevations of the Castle – except the baroque one on the Vistula side – were unfortunately modified.

On 27 February, 1861, during a demonstration staged by the Warsaw people in Castle Square, rifle salvos killed five demonstrators, shocking the whole of Polish society. On 8 April, 1861, in a clash between the population and troops, more than a hundred persons from among the workers and the poor people of Warsaw were killed.

In 1915, the Germans took over the Castle to house the offices of the German governor-general there. The Society for the Protection of the Monuments of the Past then took the Castle under its protection.

After regaining independence, the Council of Ministers passed, on 19 February, 1920, a decree on the strength of which the Royal Castle, the Palace Under the Tin Roof, Łazienki, Belweder, Wawel and Spała became the reception edifices of the Polish Republic. After 1926 the Castle became the residence of the President of the Republic. The conservation work undertaken in 1918 restored the former appear-

21. *The Castle and the Column of Sigismund III in 1938*

ance to the Stanislaus apartments and the renaissance chambers and rehabilitated the whole Castle. The original appearance was also restored in the Senate Hall by removing the built-in ceiling and walls, although its interior decoration had not been finished by the outbreak of World War Two.

Owing to the Soviet Union, which returned the works of art and historic relics, once taken away by the Tsarist authorities, it was possible to decorate the Stanislaus apartments. It was decided to pass to Wawel the Jagiellonian Arras tapestry, which had been in Warsaw from the early 17th century until the third partition and were now returned by the Soviet Union; however, a few were kept to decorate the Warsaw Castle. The imposing portrait of Stefan Czarniecki, painted in 1659 by the Danish painter Brodero Matthisen, purchased in Berlin for the Castle, was included in the Castle collections. From the palace of the Tyszkiewicz family at Landwarów, ornate doors were bought which had once been hung at the Govona palace near Turin, the property of the Torlonia Counts.

The furnishing, for example of the renaissance chambers, was completed with purchases of furniture and works of art. The Castle regained its former splendour. Until the outbreak of the war the historic rooms of the Castle were accessible to visitors. State ceremonies were also held here.

On 17 September, 1939, the Germans began to bombard the Castle with incendiary shells. On the same day, after a fire, the roof collapsed over the great Ballroom and Bacciarelli's ceiling painting burned. The workers of the National Museum and the Municipal Authorities, helped by hundreds of inhabitants of the Old Town salvaged the Castle and the cultural objects stored in it until the surrender of Warsaw. On Hitler's orders, the Castle was vandalized and looted in October, November and December 1939. In the groundfloor walls, on the outside and the inside, the German sappers drilled 10 000 holes for dynamite charges. They blew up the bare walls of the Castle only after the Warsaw Uprising.

Despite the looting and destruction, so much was left from the Royal Castle in Warsaw that it is possible to reconstruct it fully. On the site, the gothic cellars, the Town (Grodzka) Tower, the already rehabilitated King's Library, the Palace Under the Tin Roof, the walls on the side of the Vistula and the terraces on its escarpment, have survived.

After the war, the Castle grounds were dominated by the shell of the wall in full height. The opening in the first floor was the window of the Conference Closet at the Throne Hall, that in the second floor was the window of a room where Stefan Żeromski used to live and work, and where he died in 1925.

There are not only the prewar architectural designs and three thousand photographs, but also a few thousand architectural and sculpted pieces, more than three hundred salvaged paintings, more than sixty sculptures, sixteen fireplaces, hundreds of pieces of furniture, works of decorative art and historic relics. As a result of this, it was not only possible to reconstruct the Castle with complete accuracy in its previous state, but also it is to a large extent authentic.

22. *View towards the Castle from Mariensztat before 1939, on the left: St Ann's Bernardine church*

# The Reconstruction of the Royal Castle

*Aleksander Gieysztor*

The idea of rebuilding the Castle was proposed after the liberation, when the Old and New Towns were to be restored, together with other most valuable historic complexes of Warsaw. From the very beginning, the raising of the Castle from ruin was a public matter. The rebuilding of its walls was something more than the conservation of the surviving fragments. From the beginning, this undertaking was understood to be a national duty. The Castle, which had been destroyed with premeditation as a symbol of Polish statehood and culture, was to be reborn as evidence to their full vitality.

The preparatory work was begun as early as 1945, bearing in mind not only the ideological and artistic values of the Castle, but also the fact that large amounts of fragments, equipment and ample architectural, iconographic and photographic documentation survived. The experience and memory of the outstanding experts on the Castle were also utilized. In 1946, the architectural team of Jan Dąbrowski began meticulous design work. A year later the Castle grounds were partly cleared, all pieces of stone sculpture were salvaged and sometimes fragments of wainscoting were uncovered. From the preserved stone blocks, as a signal to start the work, the Town (Grodzka) Tower was restored. The Palace Under the Tin Roof was also rebuilt.

On 2 May, 1949, the Parliament called on the Government to raise the Castle from ruin. Another design was proposed, but this neglected the conservation requirements, as it put forth the idea of including modern architecture here. Soon these designs were rejected in favour of a complete return to the principles of restoration. Another draft design of the reconstruction was worked out by a team of competent architects, headed by Jan Zachwatowicz, devoted to the cause of the Castle. A monograph, which has not been published, edited by Stanisław Lorentz, was also written to supplement the design. Field work was carried out, including archaeologists. Under the dilligent care of Aleksander Król, authentic Castle relics still continued to be uncovered. However, despite the establishing of another team supervised by Jan Bogusławski, gradually silence fell over the fate of the Castle. In 1964 its grounds were cleared to form a peculiarly conceived permanent ruin. In 1965 work was finished on the conservation of an underground room discovered beneath the garden near the King's Library, in 1966 the Library was rebuilt, finally the Little Court (8, Castle Square) was rebuilt to house flats and so was Bacciarelli's atelier, to be used as the Palace of Weddings. The community of art historians and architects still had research work on their minds. Despite many obstacles, Stanisław Lorentz appealed for the reconstruction.

20th January, 1971, brought the right decision: to have the project implemented by means of voluntary work. The Citizens' Committee for the Reconstruction of the Royal Castle in Warsaw was founded. An appeal was addressed to Poles at home and abroad, expressing the will to reproduce the Castle and the conviction that *it will become, as it was in the past centuries, a monument linking the past, present and future generations of Poles, evidence to the continuity of the national history.* A few public committees, and soon the administrative Executive Board of the Castle, were established.

Under the supervision of the general designer, Jan Bogusławski, the architectural design was made by the architects of the State Enterprise of The Monument Conservation Workshops. This enterprise carried out the design and reconstruction in cooperation with a large number of design offices and institutions all over Poland. From 1971 on, the main architectural designers were Irena Oborska and Mieczysław Samborski. From the very beginning, all the designs were considered by the Architectural-Conservation Commission of the Citizens' Committee, headed by Jan Zachwatowicz, almost until his death in 1983. The members of the Commission deserving particular credit included Piotr Biegański, Jacek Cydzik, Jan Dąbrowski and Mieczysław Kuzma.

The construction work was preceded by archaeological excavations, as a result of which knowledge was gained on the building previous to the emergence of the Vasa pentagon and a large number of valuable historic objects of material and artistic culture were acquired. The assumptions which were observed in the work on the reconstruction of the Castle consisted in keeping the former outline of the building and its horizontal foundation and in integrating the preserved elements of the walls and decoration into the reconstructed solid. The principle of retaining the preserved walls of the Castle was also followed with respect to the foundations, which were replaced only in excessively damaged parts. The cellars were deepened and widened so as to house installations in them of as high a technical level as possible.

The reconstruction of the walls, while keeping everywhere possible the old masonry brick technique, offered difficulties related to the scarce number of master bricklayers who knew the manner of timbering the rib vaulting over the cellars and part of the groundfloor. These difficulties, and also others in the field of disappearing crafts, were overcome. The reproduced gothic brick was used in the façade of the Great Court. It is known from 17th-century iconographic sources that on the roof in the west façade there were small towers at corners, and between them there were four lucarnes, which were missing in the prewar Castle. One of the forms of coping the Town (Grodzka) Tower, known from iconography, was selected: it was treated as a projection of the south wing at the same height as that of the roof of the Castle. Each of the elevations offerred specific construction problems, such as the question of their stone-sculpted decoration, which used to be made from dolomite and rare sandstones, now difficult to obtain, therefore it was necessary to reopen the quarry near Szydłowiec, long out of service.

The restoration of the pre – 1939 state of the castle, carried out on the basis of the preserved fragments of equipment and research documentation, mainly applied to the Stanislaus halls on the first floor and the Jagiellonian and Vasa groundfloors. The reconstruction of the interiors with the former proportions, divisions and forms, including the modifications of decoration, covered in turn the Marble Room, nonexistent before the War in its original Vasa form, the Green and Yellow Rooms, and the Rooms of the Count Stanislaus whose 18th-century decoration was missing before the destruction of the Castle. This also applies to the Parliament Halls in the west wing, where the preserved Saxon designs made it possible for the Senators' Hall to acquire decoration close to that seen during the passing of the Third of May Constitution.

In keeping with predictions, the building was finished without decoration in 1974; in the next years tedious work was carried out on its external and internal decoration. In 1984, the interiors were ready to be furnished as a museum, except the Assembly Hall, and to receive visitors in almost a hundred rooms. One should credit with this work a huge number of workers of a variety of construction specialties, also craftsmen, artists, conservators, historians and art historians. Some branches of artistic crafts were reborn.

The returning of the Castle to life was made possible by the generosity of hundreds of thousands of Poles who answered the appeal of the Citizens' Committee for the Reconstruction. Since 1971 almost a million zloties and about 820 000 dollars has been collected. This covered the costs of the reconstruction without drawing on the budget of the state. Further contributions, necessary for the reconstruction to be finished, are still coming in. In addition to the money given by the Poles at home and abroad, and by the foreigners, friends of the Castle, one should appreciate the enormous work carried out by citizens, enterprises and schools in the first stage of the reconstruction. On a volunteer basis, work was then done, worth 36 million zloties. Since the beginning of the reconstruction, a team of a dozen retired Warsaw people has assisted it by keeping the records of the contributions, by collecting a bibliography and documentation. It is necessary to mention the many valuable gifts, including works of art presented to the Castle by individual persons, national and foreign institutions, and also by foreign governments. The number of gifts has exceeded 7000 items; the contributors have included more than 700 Polish citizens at home, 74 national institutions, 120 persons abroad (mainly of Polish origin), and 11 foreign institutions and 13 foreign governments.

Among the gifts, sometimes of very high quality, included in the Castle collections, one should mention that in 1967 the writer Ludwik Hieronim Morstin endowed in his will for the Castle the portrait of Jan Andrzej Morstin, the Grand Treasurer of

the Crown and a poet, the work by Hyacinthe Rigaud, which his family gave to the Castle after the decision to reconstruct it was proclaimed.

The foreign contributors have included the Soviet Union (e.g. an Arras tapestry from the Jagiellonian series), the German Democratic Republic (a set of Saxon furniture and paintings and Far Eastern 18th-century china), the German Federal Republic (a collection of about 50 works of 16th–18th century art); the governments of France, Sweden, Great Britain, Austria, the Netherlands, by donating valuable artistic objects have also added to the splendour of the Castle interiors. In an area of 560 m², the exhibition "The Acquisitions of the Royal Castle, a Choice of Gifts and Purchases in 1971–1982" showed the most important of them. Gifts which enrich the Castle artistically still continue to come in.

The work of the reconstruction of the Castle in the outline of its main edifice has been patronized by the Citizens' Committee for the Reconstruction of the Royal Castle in Warsaw, with the broader membership of 1981. On behalf of the Committee, the Board of Curators, headed by Stanisław Lorentz, has prepared the programme of interior decoration. In late 1980, the Management of the Royal Castle was established, whose tasks include the full museum equipment, the collection of artistic collections and documentation, research work and the

popularization of the values protected at the Castle, the direction of the further reconstruction and conservation work, including that in the direct surroundings of the Castle.

The reconstructed Royal Castle in Warsaw, a monument of national history and culture, speaks with the voice of a faithful witness. The reanimation of the architectural shape of the Castle and its interior, the preparation of its numerous rooms for receiving artistic goods and the integration of it with the cultural life of contemporary Poland have been accompanied by work on the programme of its interior decoration.

The decision made as to what the reconstructed Castle should be consists firstly in the restitution of its architectural form, secondly, in the reproduction of its ideological contents. This can be achieved by the most careful possible equipment of the Castle interior as a great sequence of former reception, official and living rooms. They represent the functions of the Castle of His Majesty the King and the Commonwealth, as its proud name once was, reproduced on the basis of historical sources while retaining the preserved and complemented elements of the decoration.

What has arisen is an imposing museum of castle interiors, conceived of in such

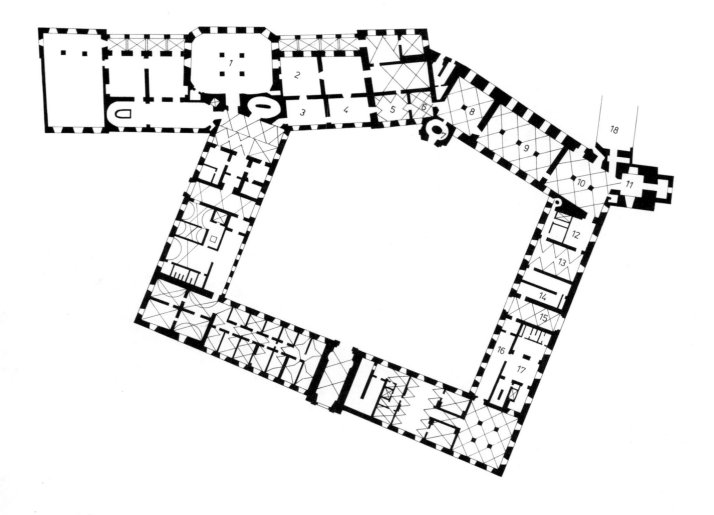

25. Plan of the Castle – groundfloor: 1 – Treasury, 2 – Vestibule to the Vistula, 3 – First Chamber, 4 – Second Chamber, 5 – Third Chamber, 6 – Vestibule of the Ladies of the Court, 7 – Ladislaus Tower, 8 – Single-Pillar Chamber, 9 – Former Delegates' Chamber, 10 – Former Delegates' Vestibule or the Two-Pillar Chamber, 11 – Chamber in the Town Tower, 12 – Officers' Vestibule, 13 – Former Guardhouse, 14 – Mier Staircase, 15 – Town Gate, 16 – Town Porch, 17 – Town Cloakroom, 18 – King's Library

a way as to respect and bring out the tradition of its former user. In forming some suites of halls, care was taken, in order to complement a tradition which had been broken or only partly confirmed, to make sure that the painted, sculpted and goldsmith's works exhibited there, did not go beyond the essential artistic canon. It is the instruction and education within the Polish historical and cultural tradition, and also the showing of its position in world culture.

In addition to its museum function of storing, conservation and making accessible works of the art of former ages, in addition to artistic references and aesthetic sensibility, the Castle interiors should also satisfy another function. This function follows from the tradition of the state sovereignty of this place – i.e. state and social functions. Cultural life should also be introduced here by way of high-rank artistic, social and scientific manifestations.

In addition to its permanent exhibition, the Castle offers temporary exhibitions, such as (in 1982/1983) the show of gifts and purchases of works of art, mentioned above, such as "The Castle in the Warsaw Uprising". In 1983, for three months, the exhibition "The Commonwealth at the Time of John III", staged in cooperation with the Main Archives of Historical Documents and the National Library, was shown. In turn, in the summer and early autumn of 1984, there was the exhibition

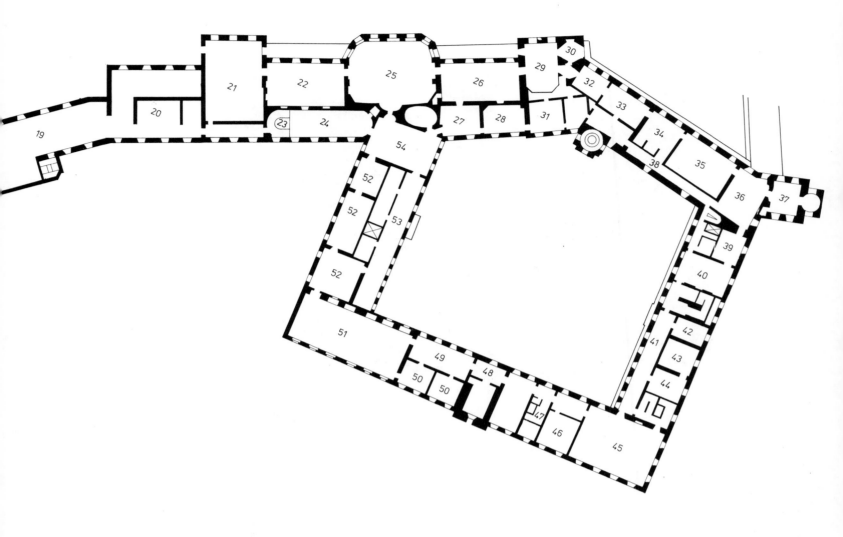

26. Plan of the Castle – first floor: 19 – SPAF Gallery, 20 – Palace of Weddings, 21 – Concert Hall, 22 – Council Hall, 23 – stairway, 24 – Oval Gallery, 25 – Assembly Hall, 26 – Knights' Hall, 27 – Marble Room, 28 – Yellow Room, 29 – Throne Hall, 30 – Conference Closet, 31 – Green Room, 32 – King's Writing Study, 33 – King's Dressing Room, 34 – King's Bedroom, 35 – Former Audience Room, 36 – Senators' Antechamber or the Canaletto Hall, 37 – Sanctuary (Chapel), 38 – Red Corridor, 39 – Officers' Antechamber, 40 – Crown Horse Guard Hall, 41 – Gallery of the Four Seasons, 42 – Apartment of the Prince Stanislaus – Study, 43 – Apartment of the Prince Stanislaus – Salon, 44 – Apartment of the Prince Stanislaus – Antechamber, 45 – New Delegates' Chamber, 46 – Vestibule to the New Delegates' Chamber, 47 – Vestibule, 48 – Little Guard Gallery, 49 – Guard Gallery, 50 – Marshall's Rooms, 51 – Senators' Hall, 52 – Prince's Rooms, 53 – Prince's Rooms, 54 – Antechamber to the Great Assembly Hall

at the King's Library, "The Constitutions in the Polish State", in cooperation with the Executive Board of the State Archives, and in particular with the Main Archives of Historical Documents and the Archives of Modern Documents. In 1985 the exhibition *Zamość Yesterday, Today and Tomorrow* was shown, and on the 125th anniversary of Ignacy Paderewski, a presentation devoted to the memory of this artist and statesman was held.

The furnishing of the Castle requires the use of many historic treasures, and also complementary reconstructed items, which, balanced in terms of number, pattern and execution, permit the Castle to function as a museum of interiors and as a place of reception. Works of art of former periods are the fundamental, and numerically predominant, part of the furnishings. They come from the prewar Castle, in particular in the case of the Stanislaus apartments. Another part of the furnishings was provided by retrievals of the Castle possessions, sometimes lost very early, and now returned by way of gifts or purchases. Another part consisted of other acquisitions, gifts or purchases, including both Polish-made objects or those related to Poland, and also others worthy of the Castle. A very large number of objects comes from the collections of the National Museum in Warsaw. Other Polish museums have also added to the achievement. The Castle still welcomes every

ELEMENTUM MEUM LIBERTAS

gesture of good will, in order to enhance its collections with gifts, deposits and purchases.

*27. Polish Eagle from the 18th century*

As in the castle's forerunner, that more ancient monument of Polish culture, the Wawel, there is one of the most imposing exhibitions of historic painting, sculpture and decorative art in Poland, a collection which is growing. It stands amongst European museum residences as the Polish national museum of castle interiors.

Again, the majesty of the former Commonwealth, its statehood and culture radiates from the restored rooms of the Royal Castle in Warsaw, the carrier of the Polish cultural identity, evidenced in the many centuries of the history of the nation. It is legitimate to use to refer to the work of the restoration of the Castle and the new service undertaken by it, to the public effort contributed to this great matter, the words of Sigismund Augustus, contained in his will of 1572: *We give and grant all these legacies to one Commonwealth, but only to the common need, not to some other, and to a common, needed and honest person.*

# Colour
# illustrations

77. Second Chamber at the Royal Castle. A Dutch-type box from the mid-16th century. A portrait of the Cardinal Jerzy Radziwiłł, by a Polish painter, after 1593

78. Second Chamber at the Royal Castle. An Italian box from the second half of the 16th century. Over the box, a portrait of Alberto Bolognetti, the Papal nuncio to Poland from 1581 on, by Federico Barocci, 1583–1585

79. Third Chamber at the Royal Castle. A wardrobe, France, second half of the 16th century. A renaissance chair, Germany, first quarter of the 17th century. Two Arras tapestries from the series "Roman Wars": "Breaking Down of the Town Gates" and "Burning of a Body", Flanders, second half of the 16th century

80. Vestibule to the Vistula at the Royal Castle. A baroque wardrobe, Netherlands, second half of the 17th century. Fire pokers and shovels, Flanders, first half of the 17th century. A still life over the fireplace, by Cornelius Norbertus Gysbrechts, 1659

81. Main Chamber at the Royal Castle

82. Main Chamber at the Royal Castle

83. Main Chamber at the Royal Castle. A cassapanca bench, Italy, the second half of the 16th century. A portrait of Ann Jagiellonian, by a Polish painter, second half of the 16th century

84. Main Chamber at the Royal Castle. A vargueño-type sepet, Spain (?), first half of the 18th century. A sepet base, Spain (?), 17th century. A portrait of Bona Sforza, by a Polish painter, second half of the 16th century

85. Dark Vestibule at the Royal Castle. Two wall benches, Florence, second half of the 16th century. In the Diagonal Vestibule – a box, Germany, about 1600

86. Single-Pillar Chamber from the Former Delegates' Chambers at the Royal Castle. A filing cabinet, Florence, about the middle of the 16th century. The painting represents the geneological tree of the Legnica-Brzeg Piasts, by a Silesian painter, after 1707

87. Former Delegates' Chamber at the Royal Castle. Gobelin verdure "Fighting Beasts", Flanders, second half of the 16th century. An armachair, Italy, the 16th/17th centuries

88. Former Delegates' Vestibule at the Royal Castle. Two Arras tapestries from the series "Hunting and Garden Games", Flanders, Audenarde, end of the 16th century. Armchair with plant-figured upholstery, France, c. 1650

89. Former Delegates' Vestibule from the Chamber at the Town Tower of the Royal Castle

90. Former Delegates' Vestibule at the Royal Castle, detail of the interior

91. Chamber in the Town Tower of the Royal Castle. Portraits of Sigismund Augustus and Archduke Karl Habsburg, father-in-law of Sigismund III

92. Chamber in the Town Tower of the Royal Castle. A portrait of John Casimir, by Peter Denckers de Rij, 1635–1648

93. Officers' Vestibule or the Middle Chamber at the Royal Castle. The Gobelin tapestry "Flowers in Vases", Netherlands, mid-17th century. A table, Italy, end of the 16th century. A portrait over the fireplace of the Prince Sigismund Casimir Vasa, by a Polish painter, first half of the 17th century

94. Detail of the Gobelin tapestry, from the Officers' Vestibule at the Royal Castle, Netherlands, mid-17th century

95. A portrait of Stefan Czarniecki, by Brodero Matthisen, 1659

96. Former Guardhouse at the Royal Castle. A trunk candlestick, gilded bronze, 17th century

97. Verdure with a water mill, France, Aubusson, first half of the 18th century

98. A bust of Ann the Austrian, wife of Louis XIII, King of France from 1615, by the sculptor Gilles Guerin, 1635–1640

99. Concert Hall at the Royal Castle. A statue of "Apollo", by André Le Brun, after 1778

100. Council Hall at the Royal Castle

101. Oval Gallery at the Royal Castle. On the left: a bust of Giovanni Pesaro, by the sculptor Giustro Le Court, Italy, second half of the 17th century; on the right: a bust of the Pope Innocent XIII, by the sculptor Pietro Bracci, after 1724

102. A portrait of Stanislaus Augustus, by Marcello Bacciarelli

103. Ball Room (Assembly Hall) at the Royal Castle

104. "Chronos" at the Knights' Hall of the Royal Castle, by the sculptor Giacomo Monaldi, 1784–1786

105. Knights' Hall at the Royal Castle, the painting on the left: "Union of Lublin" by M. Bacciarelli

106. A statue of "Fame" at the Knights' Hall of the Royal Castle, by the sculptor André Le Brun, about 1770

107. The overdoor at the Knights' Hall of the Royal Castle – a portrait of Jan Karol Chodkiewicz, by Marcello Bacciarelli, 1782

108. Marble Room at the Royal Castle

109. Marble Room at the Royal Castle, general view

110. Marble Room at the Royal Castle, detail

111. A portrait of Stephen Bathory from the Marble Cabinet of the Royal Castle, by Marcello Bacciarelli

112. Marble Room at the Royal Castle. A portrait of Stanislaus Augustus, by Marcello Bacciarelli

113. Ceiling painting by Marcello Bacciarelli at the Royal Castle in Warsaw representing "Fame Glorifying the Acts of Polish Monarchs", reconstructed by Jan Karczewski and Stefan Garwatowski

114. Throne Hall at the Royal Castle

115. Throne Hall at the Royal Castle, detail of the original batten

116. The throne chair of Stanislaus Augustus, designed by Jan Chrystian Kamsetzer, Poland, second half of the 18th century

117. Throne Hall or the New Audience Hall at the Royal Castle

118. Top of the console-table at the Throne Hall of the Royal Castle, decorated by the mosaic technique,

28. Stare Miasto i Zamek Królewski
The Old Town and the Royal Castle
La Vieille Ville et le Château Royal
La Ciudad Vieja y el Castillo Real
Die Altstadt und das Königsschloß
Старый Город и Королевский замок

30. Plac Zamkowy
Castle Square
La Place du Château
La Plaza del Castillo
Der Schloßplatz
Замковая площадь

29. Plac Zamkowy z kolumną Zygmunta III
Castle Square with the Column of Sigismund III
La Place du Château avec la colonne de Sigismond III
La Plaza del Castillo con la columna de Zygmunt III
Der Schloßplatz mit der Sigismund III.-Säule
Замковая площадь с колонной Сигизмунду III

**33.** Ulica Piwna przy placu Zamkowym
Piwna Street at Castle Square
La rue Piwna à son débouché sur la place du Château
La calle Piwna a la Plaza del Castillo
Die Piwna-Straße am Schloßplatz
Впуск улицы Пивной на Замковую площадь

**34.** Plac Zamkowy z wlotem ulicy Piwnej
Castle Square with Piwna Street
La place du Château avec l'entrée de la rue Piwna
La Plaza del Castillo con la entrada de la calle Piwna
Der Schloßplatz mit Auslauf der Piwna-Straße
Замковая площадь с впуском улицы Пивной

**36.** Ulica Jezuicka
Jezuicka Street
La rue Jezuicka
La calle Jezuicka
Die Jesuiten-Straße
Улица Иезуитская

**5.** Dachy Starego Miasta
Roofs of the Old Town
Toits de la Vieille Ville
Tejados de la Ciudad Vieja
Dächer der Altstadt
Крыши Старого Города

37. Ulica Kanonia
    Kanonia Street
    La rue Kanonia
    La calle Kanonia
    Die Kanonia-Straße
    Улица Канония

**38.** Kamieniczki na ulicy Kanonia
Houses in Kanonia Street
Petites maisons de la rue Kanonia
Casas de piedra en la calle Kanonia
Bürgerhäuser in der Kanonia-Straße
Дома на улице Канония

39. Wywieszka salonu kosmetycznego „Izis"
Signboard of the "Izis" beauty parlour
Enseigne du salon de beauté «Izis»
El anuncio del salón de belleza «Izis»
Aushängeschild des Kosmetiksalons „Izis"
Вывеска косметического зала „Изис" на улице Пивной

40. Ulica Piwna
Piwna Street
La rue Piwna
La calle Piwna
Die Piwna-Straße
Улица Пивна

1. Ulica Piekarska
Piekarska Street
La rue Piekarska
La calle Piekarska
Die Piekarska-Straße
Улица Пекарска

42. Kamienica „Pod św. Anną" od ulicy Wąski Dunaj
St Anne House from Wąski Dunaj Street
La maison «A Ste-Anne» du côté de la rue Wąski Dunaj
La casa de piedra «Bajo la Santa Ana» desde la calle Wąski Dunaj
Das Bürgerhaus „Unter der hl. Anna"
Дом под св. Анной от стороны улицы Узкий Дунай

43. Wywieszka apteki staromiejskiej
Signboard of the Old Town pharmacy
Enseigne de pharmacie dans la Vieille Ville
El anuncio de la farmacia de la Ciudad Vieja
Aushängeschild der Altstadtapotheke
Аптечная вывеска

Fragment elewacji kamienicy staromiejskiej
Detail of the elevation of an Old Town house
Façade d'une maison de la Vieille Ville. Détail
Fragmento de la fachada de una casa de piedra en la Ciudad Vieja
Teil der Fassade eines Altstadtbürgerhauses
Фрагмент полихромной отделки одного из домов Старого Города

**45.** Katedra św. Jana
St John's cathedral
La Cathédrale St-Jean
La catedral de San Juan
Die St.-Johann-Kathedrale
Кафедральный собор св. Яна

46. Stare Miasto od strony Wisły
The Old Town from the Vistula
La Vieille Ville vue de la Vistule
La Ciudad Vieja vista desde la parte del Vistula
Die Altstadt von der Weichselseite
Старый Город от стороны Вислы

47. Stare Miasto od strony ulicy Bugaj
The Old Town from Bugaj Street
La Vieille Ville vue de la rue Bugaj
La Ciudad Vieja vista desde la calle Bugaj
Die Altstadt von der Bugaj-Straße
Старый Город от стороны улицы Бугай ▷

**48.** Rynek Starego Miasta, strona Kołłątaja
The Old Town Market Place, Kołłątaj Side
La Place du Marché de la Vieille Ville, côté Kołłątaj
La Plaza de la Ciudad Vieja, la parte de Kołłątaj
Der Altstadtmarkt, die Kołłątaj-Seite
Рынок Старого Города, сторона Коллонтая

**49.** Wywieszka kawiarni „Krokodyl"
Signboard of the "Krokodyl" Café
Enseigne du café «Krokodyl»
El anuncio de la cafetería «Krokodyl»
Aushängeschild des Cafés „Krokodyl"
Вывеска кафе „Крокодил"

Rynek Starego Miasta, strona Barssa
The Old Town Market Place, Barss Side
La Place du Marché de la Vieille Ville, côté Barss
La Plaza de la Ciudad Vieja, la parte de Barss
Der Altstadtmarkt, die Barss-Seite
Рынок Старого Города – сторона Барсса

**50.** Kamienica Fukiera na Rynku Starego Miasta
Fukier House in the Old Town Market Place
La Maison Fukier sur La Place du Marché de la Vieille Ville
La casa de piedra de Fukier en la Plaza de la Ciudad Vieja
Das Fugger-Bürgerhaus am Altstadtmarkt
Дом Фукера на Рынке Старого Города

52. Muzeum Historyczne m. Warszawy
The Historical Museum of the City of Warsaw
Le Musée historique de Varsovie
Museo Histórico de la Ciudad de Varsovia
Das Historische Museum der Stadt Warschau
Исторический музей города Варшавы

53. Kur Bractwa Strzeleckiego, 1552 r.
 The cock of the Shooting Club, 1552
 Coq de la Confrérie des Tireurs, 1552
 El gallo de la Congregación de los Tiradores, 1552
 Hahn der Schützengilde, 1552
 Кур Братства Стрелков, 1552 год

54. Rynek Starego Miasta
The Old Town Market Place
La Place du Marché de la Vieille Ville
La Plaza de la Ciudad Vieja
Der Altstadtmarkt
Рынок Старого Города

56. Ulica Krzywe Koło
Krzywe Koło Street
La rue Krzywe Koło
La calle Krzywe Koło
Die Krzywe Koło-Straße
Улица Кривое Коло

55. Rynek Starego Miasta, strona Dekerta
The Old Town Market Place, Dekert Side
La Place du Marché de la Vieille Ville, côté Dekert
La Plaza de la Ciudad Vieja, la parte de Dekert
Der Altstadtmarkt, die Dekert-Seite
Рынок Старого Города – сторона Декерта

57–58. Barbakan
The Barbican
La Barbacane
La Barbacana
Die Barbakane
Барбакан

59. Ulica Brzozowa
Brzozowa Street
La rue Brzozowa
La calle Brzozowa
Die Brzozowa-Straße
Улица Березовая ▷

60. Mury obronne Starego Miasta
The defensive walls of the Old Town
Les remparts de la Vieille Ville
Muros de defensa de la Ciudad Vieja
Schutzmauer der Altstadt
Оборонные стены Старого Города

61. Widok ogólny Nowego Miasta
A general view of the New Town
Vue générale de la Ville Neuve
Vista general de la Ciudad Nueva
Gesamtansicht der Neustadt
Общий вид Нового Города

62. Ulica Mostowa
Mostowa Street
La rue Mostowa
La calle Mostowa
Die Mostowa-Straße
Улица Мостова

63. Rynek Nowego Miasta i kościół Sakramentek
The New Town Market with the church of the Holy Sacrament
La Place du Marché de la Ville Neuve et l'église des Dames-du-St-Sacrement
La Plaza de la Ciudad Nueva y la iglesia de las Sacramentos
Der Neustadtmarkt und die Kirche der Sakramentsschwestern
Рынок Нового Города и костёл Сакраменток

64. Nowe Miasto od strony Wisły
The New Town from the Vistula
La Ville Neuve vue de la Vistule
La Nueva Ciudad vista desde la parte del Vistula
Die Neustadt von der Weichselseite
Новый Город от стороны Вислы

**65.** Kościół Nawiedzenia NMP na Nowym Mieście
The church of the Most Blessed Virgin Mary in the New Town
L'église de la Visitation de la Sainte Vierge dans la Ville Neuve
La iglesia de la Visitación de Nuestra Señora en la Ciudad Nueva
Die Kirche der Allerheiligsten Jungfrau Maria in der Neustadt
Новый Город. Костёл Навещения Святой Марии Девы

**66.** Widok na Stare Miasto od strony Wisłostrady
View of the Old Town from the Wisłostrada Highway
La Vieille Ville vue du boulevard longeant la Vistule
Vista de la Ciudad Vieja desde la Autopista del Vistula
Die Altstadt von der Verkehrsstraße Wisłostrada aus gesehen
Вид Старого Города от стороны Вислострады

Plac Zamkowy
Castle Square
La Place du Château
La Plaza del Castillo
Der Schloßplatz
Замковая площадь

**68.** Zamek Królewski i Stare Miasto
View of the Royal Castle and the Old Town
Le Château Royal et la Vieille Ville
El Castillo Real y la Ciudad Vieja
Das Königsschloß und die Altstadt
Вид Королевского замка и Старого Города

70. Plac Zamkowy i Zamek Królewski
Castle Square and the Royal Castle
La Place du Château et le Château Royal
La Plaza del Castillo y el Castillo Real
Der Schloßplatz und das Königsschloß
Королевский замок и Замковая площадь

9. Zamek Królewski z ulicy Świętojańskiej
View of the Royal Castle from Świętojańska Street
Le Château Royal vu de la rue Świętojańska
El Castillo Real visto desde la calle Świętojańska
Ansicht des Königsschlosses von der Świętojańska-Straße
Вид Королевского замка от стороны улицы Свентоянской

71. Zamek Królewski i kolumna Zygmunta III
The Royal Castle and the Column of Sigismund III
Le Château Royal et la colonne de Sigismond III
El Castillo Real y la Columna de Zygmunt III
Das Königsschloß und die Sigismund III.-Säule
Королевский замок и колонна Сигизмунду III

73. Elewacja gotycka na dziedzińcu zamkowym
The Gothic elevation in the castle court
Façade gothique du Château côté cour
Fachada gótica en el patio del Castillo
Gotische Fassade von der Seite des Schloßinnenhofs
Готическая отделка в замковом двору

74. Piwnica Książęca
The Prince's Cellar
La Cave princière
Sótano Principesco
Der Herzogliche Keller
Княжеский подвал

75–76. Komnata Przednia
Front Chamber
Première Chambre
Cuarto Delantero
Das Vordergemach
Передняя комната

77–78. Komnata Wtóra
Second Chamber
Deuxième Chambre
Cuarto Segundo
Das Zweite Gemach
Покой второй

79. Komnata Trzecia
Third Chamber
Troisième Chambre
Cuarto Tercero
Das Dritte Gemach
Покой третий

80. Sień ku Wiśle
Vestibule to the Vistula
Vestibule donnant sur la Vistule
Vestíbulo hacía el Vistula
Ein zur Weichsel gerichteter Flur
Сени к Висле

81–82. Komnata Główna
Main Chamber
Chambre Principale
Cuarto Principal
Das Hauptgemach
Главный зал

83–84. Komnata Główna
Main Chamber
Chambre Principale
Cuarto Principal
Das Hauptgemach
Главный зал ▷

85. Sień Ciemna
   Dark Vestibule
   Le Vestibule obscur
   Vestíbulo Obscuro
   Der Dunkle Flur
   Темная сень

86. Izba Jednosłupowa z Dawnych Komnat Poselskich
Single-Pillar Chamber of the Former Delegates' Chambers
Salle à un pilier des Anciennes Salles des Députés
Cuarto de una Columna de los Antiguos Cuartos de Diputados
Das Ein-Pfeiler-Gemach aus den Alten Abgeordnetengemächern
Зал с одной колонной, один из бывших посольских залов

87. Dawna Izba Poselska
Former Delegates' Chamber
Ancienne Chambre des Députés
Antigua Sala de Diputados
Die Alte Abgeordnetenkammer
Бывший Посольский зал

88. Dawna Sień Poselska
    Former Delegates' Vestibule
    Ancien Vestibule des Députés
    Antiguo Vestíbulo de Diputados
    Der Alte Abgeordnetenflur
    Бывшая Посольская лестница

89–90. Dawna Sień Poselska
Former Delegates' Vestibule
Ancien Vestibule des Députés
Antiguo Vestíbulo de Diputados
Der Alte Abgeordnetenflur
Бывшая Посольская лестница

92. Portret króla Jana Kazimierza, 1635–1648
Portrait of king John Casimir, 1635–1648
Portrait du roi Jean-Casimir, 1635–1648
Retrato de rey Jan Kazimierz, 1635–1648
Porträt des Königs Jan Kasimir, 1635–1648
Портрет Яна Казимежа, 1635–1648 г.г.

91. Izba w Wieży Grodzkiej
Chamber in the Town Tower
Salle dans la Tour Grodzka
Cuarto en la Torre de la Ciudad
Gemach im Burgturm
Зал в Городской башне

**93.** Sień Oficerów (Izba Średnia)
Officers' Vestibule (Middle Chamber)
Le Vestibule des Officiers (Salle Moyenne)
Vestíbulo de Oficiales (Cuarto Mediano)
Der Offiziersflur (das Mittlere Gemach)
Офицерская передняя (Средний зал)

**94.** Gobelin w Sieni Oficerów, poł. XVII w.
Gobelin tapestry in the Officers' Vestibule, mid-17th century
Tapisserie dans le Vestibule des Officiers, milieu du XVIIᵉ s.
Tapiz en el Vestíbulo de Oficiales, mitad del siglo XVII
Gobelin im Offiziersflur, Mitte des 17.Jh.
Гобелен в Офицерской передней

**95.** Portret hetmana Stefana Czarnieckiego, 1659 r.
Portrait of Commander-in-Chief Stefan Czarnied
Portrait de l'hetman Stefan Czarniecki, 1659
Retrato de Stefan Czarniecki, 1659
Porträt des Hetmans Stefan Czarniecki, 1659
Портрет Стефана Чарнецкого, 1659 год

96. Dawna Kordegarda
Former Guardhouse
L'ancien Corps de Garde
Antiguo Cuerpo de Guardia
Die Alte Wachstube
Бывшая кордегардия

**97.** Gobelin z 1 poł. XVII w.

Gobelin tapestry from the 1st half of the 17th century

Tapisserie de la première moitié du XVII $^e$ s.

Tapiz de la 1ra mitad del siglo XVII

Gobelin aus der 1. Hälfte des 17.Jh.

Гобелен, первая половина XVII века

98. Popiersie Anny Austriaczki, 1635–1640
A bust of Anne the Austrian, 1635–1640
Buste d'Anne d'Autriche, 1635–1640
Busto de Ana de Austria, 1635–1640
Büste der Anna von Österreich, 1635–1640
Бюст Анны Австрийской, 1635–1640 г.г.

**101.** Galeria Owalna
Oval Gallery
La Galerie Ovale
Galería Ovalada
Die Ovale Galerie
Круглая галерея

**102.** Portret króla Stanisława Augusta, mal. M. Bacciarelli
Portrait of King Stanislaus Augustus, by M. Bacciarelli
Portrait du roi Stanislas Auguste par M. Bacciarelli
Retrato de rey Stanisław August, pintor M. Bacciarelli
Porträt des Königs Stanislaus August, gemalt von M. Bacciarelli
Портрет короля Станислава Августа кисти М. Баччарелли

CASTI DUM VITA MANEB

MART. CROMERUS
✝ MDLXXXIX.

EBO DIC

JOA.CARO.HODKIEWICZ
✝ MDCXXI

AD DELIN. IOAN. CHR. KAMSETZER. 1794
STEPH. GARWATOWSKI & IOAN. KARCZEWSKI 1982 PINX.

VENCESLAUS
BOHEMUS

VLADISLAUS
LOCTIUS

CASIMIRUS
MAGNUS

☩MCCCV.

☩MCCCXXXI.

☩MCC · CLXX ·

111. Portret króla Stefana Batorego, mal. M. Bacciarelli
Portrait of King Stephen Bathory, by M. Bacciarelli
Portrait du roi Etienne Bathory par M. Bacciarelli
Retrato de rey Stefan Batory, pintor M. Bacciarelli
Porträt des Königs Stefan Batory, gemalt von M. Bacciarelli
Портрет короля Стефана Батория кисти М. Баччарелли

112. Portret króla Stanisława Augusta, mal. M. Bacciarelli
Portrait of King Stanislaus Augustus, by M. Bacciarelli
Portrait du roi Stanislas Auguste par M. Bacciarelli
Retrato de rey Stanisław August, pintor M. Bacciarelli
Porträt des Königs Stanislaus August, gemalt von M. Bacciare
Портрет короля Станислава Августа кисти М. Баччарелли

REGUM · MEMORIA · DICAVIT
STANISLAUS · AUGUSTUS · REGE · MONUMENTUM
ANNO · DN ~                                    ~ MDCCLXXI

LUDOVICUS
HUNGARUS

MCCCLXX

HEL

113. Plafon w Pokoju Marmurowym
Plafond in the Marble Room
Plafond dans la Chambre de Marbre
Plafón en el Cuarto de Mármol
Plafond im Marmorzimmer
Плафон в Мраморной комнате

114. Sala Tronowa (Sala Audiencjonalna Nowa)
Throne Hall (New Audience Hall)
La Salle du Trône (Nouvelle Salle d'Audience)
Sala del Trono (Nueva Sala de Audiencias)
Der Thronsaal (der Neue Audienzsaal)
Тронный зал (Новый Аудиенц-зал)

115. Fragment listwy z Sali Tronowej
Detail of a batten from the Throne Hall
Listel de la Salle du Trône. Fragment
Fragmento de un listón de la Sala del Trono
Teil einer Leiste aus dem Thronsaal
Фрагмент обшивки стен Тронного зала

116. Fotel tronowy króla Stanisława Augusta
Throne chair of King Stanislaus Augustus
Trône du roi Stanislas Auguste
Butaca del trono de rey Stanisław August
Der Thronsessel vom König Stanislaus August.
Тронное кресло короля Станислава Аугуста

117. Sala Tronowa
Throne Hall
La Salle du Trône
Sala del Trono
Der Thronsaal
Тронный зал

118.
Blat stołu konsolowego w Sali Tronowej, 1780 r.
Top of the console-table in the Throne Hall, 1780
Dessus de console dans la Salle du Trône, 1780
Tabla de la mesa de consola en la Sala del Trono, 1780
Blatt des Konsolentisches im Thronsaal, 1780
Верх стола в Тронном зале, 1780 год

119–120.
Gabinet Konferencyjny obok Sali Tronowej
Conference Cabinet by the Throne Hall
Cabinet des Conférences à côté de la Salle du Trône
Gabinete de Conferencia al lado de la Sala del Trono
Das Konferenzkabinett neben dem Thronsaal
Конференц-кабинет возле Тронного зала   ▷

**121.** Portrety Fryderyka II i Katarzyny II, 2 poł. XVIII w.
Portraits of Frederick II and Catherine II, 2nd half of the 18th century
Portraits de Frédéric II et de Catherine II, seconde moitié du XVIIIᵉ s.
Retratos de Fryderyk II y de Katarzyna II, 2da mitad del siglo XVIII
Bildnisse von Friedrich II. und Katharina II., 2. Hälfte des 18.Jh.
Портреты Екатерины II и Фридриха II, вторая половина XVIII в.

**122.** Blat stolika w Gabinecie Konferencyjnym, 1777 r.
Top of the table from the Conference Cabinet, 1777
Le dessus de la petite table du Cabinet des Conférences, 1777
Tabla de la mesita del Gabinete de Conferencia, 1777
Blatt eines kleinen Tisches im Konferenzkabinett, 1777
Верх столика в Конференц-кабинете, 1777 год

123. Fragment dekoracji Gabinetu Konferencyjnego
Fragment of the decoration in the Conference Cabinet
Le Cabinet des Conférences. Fragment de la décoration
Fragmento de la decoración del Gabinete de Conferencia
Teil der Dekoration im Konferenzkabinett
Фрагмент декора Конференц-кабинета

**126–127.** Garderoba Jego Królewskiej Mości
King's Dressing Room
La Garderobe de Sa Majesté le Roi
Vestuario de Su Alteza el Rey
Der Ankleideraum Seiner Königlichen Majestät
Гардероб короля

128. Martwa natura ,,Vanitas'', ok. poł. XVII w.
Still-life ''Vanitas'', about the mid-17th century
«Vanitas», nature morte, vers le milieu du XVII$^e$ s.
Naturaleza muerta «Vanitas»', alrededor de la mitad del siglo XVII
Stilleben ,,Vanitas'', um die Mitte des 17.Jh.
Натюрморт ,,Ванитас'', ок. половины XVII века

129. Garderoba Jego Królewskiej Mości
King's Dressing Room
La Garderobe de Sa Majesté le Roi
Vestuario de Su Alteza el Rey
Der Ankleideraum Seiner Königlichen Majestä
Гардероб короля

130–131. Pokój Sypialny
King's Bedroom
La Chambre à coucher
Dormitorio
Das Schlafzimmer
Спальная комната короля

132.

Pokój Sypialny
King's Bedroom
La Chambre à coucher
Dormitorio
Das Schlafzimmer
Спальная комната короля

133.

Pokój Audiencjonalny Dawny
Former Audience Room
Ancienne Salle d'Audience
Antiguo Cuarto de Audiencias
Das Alte Audienzzimmer
Бывший Приёмный зал

134. Pokój Audiencjonalny Dawny
Former Audience Room
Ancienne Salle d'Audience
Antiguo Cuarto de Audiencias
Das Alte Audienzzimmer
Бывший Приёмный зал

135. Zegar z Pokoju Audiencjonalnego, przed 1777 r.
Clock from the Audience Room, before 1777
Horloge de la Salle d'Audience, avant 1777
Reloj del Cuarto de Audiencias, antes del año 1777
Uhr aus dem Audienzzimmer, vor 1777
Часы с бывшего Приёмного зала, до 1777 года

136. Pokój Audiencjonalny Dawny
Former Audience Room
Ancienne Salle d'Audience
Antiguo Cuarto de Audiencia
Das Alte Audienzzimmer
Бывший Приёмный зал

137. Plafon w Pokoju Audiencjonalnym
Plafond in the Audience Room
Plafond de la Salle d'Audience
Plafón en el Cuarto de Audiencias
Plafond im Audienzzimmer
Плафон в бывшем приёмном зале

138. Przedpokój Senatorski (Sala Canaletta)
Senators' Antechamber (Canaletto Hall)
Vestibule des Sénateurs (Salle Canaletto)
Antecámara de Senadores (Sala de Canaletto)
Das Senatorenvorzimmer (Canaletto-Saal)
Сенаторская передняя

139. Posadzka w Sali Canaletta
Pavement in the Canaletto Hall
Parquet de la Salle Canaletto
Piso de parquet en la Sala de Canaletto
Fußboden im Canaletto-Saal
Пол в зале Каналетто

142. Kopuła w kaplicy
Dome in the chapel
La coupole de la Chapelle
Cúpula de la Capilla
Kuppel in der Kapelle
Купол часовни

143. Przedpokój Pierwszy (Oficerski)
First, or Officers', Vestibule
Premier Vestibule (des Officiers)
Antecámara Primera (de Oficiales)
Das Erste (Offiziers-) Vorzimmer
Первая (или офицерская) передняя

144. Apartament księcia Stanisława, Antyszambra
Apartment of Prince Stanislaus, Antechamber
Appartement du prince Stanislas, l'Antichambre
Apartamento del principe Stanisław, Antecámara
Appartement des Herzogs Stanislaus, Vorzimmer
Апартамент князя Станислава

145. Gobelin w Antyszambrze, 1 poł. XIX w.
Gobelin tapestry in the Antechamber, 1st half of the 19th century
L'Antichambre. Tapisserie, première moitié du XIXᵉ s.
Tapiz en la Antecámara, 1ra mitad del siglo XIX
Gobelin im Vorzimmer, 1. Hälfte des 19.Jh.
Гобелен в антикамере, первая половина XIX века

146. Apartament księcia Stanisława, Antyszambra
Apartment of Prince Stanislaus, Antechamber
Appartement du prince Stanislas, l'Antichambre
Apartamento del principe Stanisław, Antecámara
Appartement des Herzogs Stanislaus, Vorzimmer
Апартамент князя Станислава, Антикамера

147. Apartament księcia Stanisława, Pokój Towarzyski
Apartment of Prince Stanislaus, Salon
Appartement du prince Stanislas, Chambre des Mondanités
Apartamento del principe Stanisław, Cuarto Social
Appartement des Herzogs Stanislaus, das Gesellschaftszimmer
Апартамент князя Станислава, Гостинная комната

148. Apartament księcia Stanisława, Pokój Towarzyski
Apartment of Prince Stanislaus, Salon
Appartement du prince Stanislas, Chambre des Mondanités
Apartamento del principe Stanisław, Cuarto Social
Appartement des Herzogs Stanislaus, das Gesellschaftszimmer
Апартамент князя Станислава, Гостинная комната

149. Apartament księcia Stanisława, Gabinet
Apartment of Prince Stanislaus, Cabinet
Appartement du prince Stanislas, Cabinet
Apartamento del principe Stanisław, Gabinete
Appartement des Herzogs Stanislaus, das Kabinett
Апартамент князя Станислава, Кабинет

150. Zegar w Gabinecie (Apartament księcia Stanisława), ok. 1750 r.
Clock in the Cabinet (Prince Stanislaus' Apartment), about 1750
Cabinet (Appartement du prince Stanislas). Horloge, vers 1750.
Reloj en el Gabinete, alrededor del año 1750
Uhr im Kabinett (Appartement des Herzogs Stanislaus), um 1750
Часы в Кабинете (Апартамент князя Станислава), ок. 1750 года

153. Maria Leszczyńska jako Junona, 1731 r.
Maria Leszczyńska as Juno, 1731
Maria Leszczyńska en Junon, 1731
Maria Leszczyńska como Junona, el año 1731
Maria Leszczyńska als Juno, 1731
Мария Лещинская в виде Юноны, ок. 1731 года

152. Kominek w Gabinecie (Apartament księcia Stanisława)
Fireplace in the Cabinet (Apartment of Prince Stanislaus)
Cabinet (Appartement du prince Stanislas). Cheminée
Chimenea en el Gabinete (Apartamento del principe Stanisław)
Kamin in Kabinett (Appartement des Herzogs Stanislaus)
Камин в Кабинете (Апартамент князя Станислава)

154. Gobelin, 1548–1553
Gobelin tapestry, 1548–1553
Tapisserie, 1548–1553
Tapiz, 1548–1553
Gobelin, 1548–1553
Гобелен, 1548–1553 г.г.

155. Portret Marii Józefy, ok. 1750 r.
Portrait of Mary Josephine, about 1750
Portrait de Marie-Josèphe, vers 1750
Retrato de Maria Józefa, alrededor del año 1750
Bildnis von Maria Josefa, um 1750
Портрет Марии Иосифы, ок. 1750 года

157. Posążek konny Augusta II, ok. 1830 r.
Equestrian statue of Augustus II, about 1830
Statuette équestre d'Auguste II, vers 1830
Pequeña estatua a caballo de August II, alrededor de año 1830
Kleines Reiterstandbild von August II., um 1830
Конная статуэтка Августа II, ок. 1830 года

156. „Porwanie Prozerpiny przez Plutona", koniec XVII w.
"Rape of Proserpine by Pluto", end of the 17th century
«L'Enlèvement de Proserpine par Pluton», fin du XVIIe s.
«Rapto de Prozerpina por Plutono», fines del siglo XVII
„Proserpinas Entführung durch Pluto", Ende des 17.Jh.
„Похищение Прозерпины Плутоном", конец XVII века

158. Sala Senatorska (Sala Konstytucji 3 maja)
Senators' Hall (Third of May Constitution Hall)
La Salle des Sénateurs (Salle de la Constitution du 3 Mai)
Sala de Senadores (Sala de la Constituación del 3 de Mayo)
Der Senatorensaal (der Saal der Verfassung vom 3. Mai)
Сенаторский зал (зал Конституции 3 Мая)                    ▷

**CIP – Biblioteka Narodowa**
The Old Town and the Royal Castle in
Warsaw / colour phot. by Krzysztof
Jabłoński; transl. [from Pol.] by
Jerzy A. Bałyga. – [2 ed.]. –
Warsaw: "Arkady", 1992

Arkady, Warsaw 1992
Second edition
Printed in Slovenia by Mladinska knjiga, Ljubljana
22088/1/RA/Be